BY THE PEOPLE, FOR THE PEOPLE

U.S. Government and Citizenship

DEBORAH J. SHORT

MARGARET SEUFERT-BOSCO

ALLENE GUSS GROGNET

A publication of **CAL** Center for Applied Linguistics

DELTA SYSTEMS CO., INC., ● 1400 Miller Parkway ● McHenry, IL 60050–7030

Library of Congress Cataloging-in-Publication Data

Short, Deborah.
 By the people, for the people : U.S. government and citizenship /
Deborah Short, Margaret Seufert-Bosco, Allene G. Grognet.
  p.   cm.
 "A Publication of CAL, Center for Applied Linguistics."
 ISBN 0-937354-69-4 (paper)
 1. Readers-United States. 2. English language-Textbooks for
foreign speakers. 3. United States-Politics and government.
4. Citizenship-United States. I. Seufert-Bosco, Margaret.
II. Grognet, Allene Guss. III. Center for Applied Linguistics.
IV. Title.
PE 1127.H5S49 1992
428.6'4-dc20

                                                                91-6395
                                                                   CIP

Acquisitions Editor: *Anne Riddick*
Editorial/production supervision
   and interior design: *Louise B. Capuano* and *Arthur Maisel*
Text illustrations: *D.M. Graphics, Inc.*
Cover design: *Wanda Lubelska*
Cover photo: *Barbara DeWitt/Comstock*
Pre-press buyer: *Ray Keating*
Manufacturing buyer: *Lori Bulwin*

©1992 by the Center for Applied Linguistics
Reprinted in 1995 by Delta Systems Co., Inc.
1400 Miller Parkway, McHenry, IL 60050-7030

Text photo credits appear on page 174.

Printed in the United States of America

10 9 8 7 6 5 4 3

ISBN 0-937354-69-4

Prentice-Hall International (UK) Limited, *London*
Prentice-Hall of Australia Pty. Limited, *Sydney*
Prentice-Hall Canada Inc., *Toronto*
Prentice-Hall Hispanoamericana, S.A., *Mexico*
Prentice-Hall of India Private Limited, *New Delhi*
Prentice-Hall of Japan, Inc., *Tokyo*
Simon & Schuster Asia Pte. Ltd., *Singapore*
Editora Prentice-Hall do Brasil, Ltda., *Rio de Janeiro*

Table of Contents

To the Student

We wrote this book for you. We hope you will think the lessons are interesting. We hope you will enjoy learning about the U.S. government. The lessons can help you become better residents and citizens of the U.S.

Each lesson has a title. It tells you the subject of each lesson. Under each title there will be one or more objectives. These objectives say what you will learn from the lesson.

You will practice all your English skills—listening, speaking, reading, and writing. Most of the lessons have five parts:

I. **Pre-Reading**
II. **Information**
III. **Reading**
IV. **Testing skills**
V. **Review**

I. Pre-Reading

In the first part of every lesson, **Pre-Reading,** you will find some questions to discuss with a partner, in a small group, or with the class. These questions will be about some pictures and some ideas about government.

After the discussion, you will find some new vocabulary words. Their definitions will help you understand the lesson. Some of these words have other definitions, too. Sometimes you will have a written exercise to do.

Some exercises will tell you to guess. Guessing means you do not really know the answers. You give your ideas about what you think the answer will be.

Other exercises will ask you to scan a paragraph. When you scan you do not read everything. You look for specific information. You can review your answers for the guessing and scanning exercises at the end of the lesson.

II. Information

The **Information** is always on a chart or in a diagram. It shows you the main points of each lesson.

First, think about the title. Next, read the information on the page carefully. Ask yourself questions about the information. For example, if the lesson is about the President, you can ask:

- Who is the President?
- What does the President do?
- Where does the President live?

Finally, do the exercises—*Using the Information*. Look at the Information page (and sometimes the Vocabulary) to help you complete the speaking, listening, and writing exercises.

III. Reading

The **Reading** is usually one to five paragraphs long. Sometimes the Reading will give you more information about the main points. Sometimes the Reading will give you new information.

- First, think about the title.
- Next, read the paragraphs quickly for a general idea.
- Then, read the paragraphs carefully.
- Finally, do the exercise(s)—*Using the Reading*. Look at the Reading (and sometimes the Information) to help you complete the exercise(s).

IV. Testing skills

The **Testing skills** help you test yourself. Can you answer the questions without looking at the Information and the Reading? If you cannot answer the test questions, you should look back at the Information and Reading again.

You will learn about many different types of tests. Some of the tests are oral and some are written. We included some ideas about how to answer oral questions. This section will help you prepare for the citizenship test.

V. Review

The last part of every lesson is the **Review**. The Review has the most important things for you to remember. There are usually one to five questions. If you cannot answer the review questions, you should look back at the Information and Reading again. If you can answer the review questions, you can go on to the next lesson.

What should you do if you are **not in a class?** What should you do if you are studying **alone?**

If you are studying alone, show the lessons to your friends, or someone in your family, or someone at work. Ask people to help you practice your English. Ask them to be your partner for the speaking exercises. Ask them to do the group discussions with you.

Can you use this book if you **were not** born in the U.S.? **YES!**

Can you use this book if you **were** born in the U.S.? **YES!**

This book will help everyone learn more about U.S. history and government. Sometimes you will see questions about *"your"* country. If you **were** born in the U.S., answer these questions with information about the native country of your family or friends. You can also answer these questions with information about other countries you know about.

Deborah J. Short

Margaret Seufert-Bosco

Allene Guss Grognet

Acknowledgments

The authors would like to thank the following individuals for their assistance during the preparation of this book:

Our colleagues at CAL who reviewed and edited draft versions of the book:

Ann Kennedy

JoAnn Crandall

Molly Kirby

Margo Pfleger

Don Ranard

Mary Jo Larson

Mary Schleppegrell

Other reviewers of the manuscript:

Frank Siciliano, Phoenix, AZ
Autumn Keltner, San Diego, CA
Sadae Iwataki, Los Angeles, CA
Carol Van Duzer, Washington, D.C.

Editorial and technical assistants:

Dora Johnson
Sonia Kundert

Julie Krause
Robin Schaefer

Illustrators:

Nicole Grognet
Martin Johnson

Richard Mott
Michael Dyre

Finally, we would like to thank:

Mr. Thomas Cook, Senior Immigration Examiner,
Immigration and Naturalization Service, Washington, D.C.,

for his guidance and support throughout the project.

DJS
MS-B
AGG

Glossary

Before you begin, look at the following words and definitions. These are important words you will need to understand the lessons. Ask someone to help you with these words or use your dictionary.

Citizen: If you are born in the U.S., you can be a citizen. If your parents are citizens and you are born in another country, you can be a citizen. If you are an immigrant, you can become a citizen after 3–5 years.

Constitution: A plan of government; rules for governing

Democracy: A type of government; in a democracy the people make a lot of decisions; the people vote for their leaders

Duty: A responsibility; something you have to do

(to) *Elect:* Choose by voting

Freedom: Liberty; the ability to do, say, think, or write your ideas

Judge: The person who is the head of a court; a justice

Jury: A group of citizens; they listen to a case in court and make a decision about the case

Law: Rules of a government; laws tell us things we can do and things we cannot do

Legal: Following the law

    Illegal: Not following the law

Naturalization: The process for an immigrant to become a citizen of the U.S.

Powers: Special responsibilities from the Constitution

Principles: General rules and basic ideas

Republican form of government: Like a democratic government; usually has a head of state (for example, a president); the citizens elect officials to represent their interests

Resident Alien (Permanent Resident):   An immigrant with a green card; someone with legal permission to live and work in the U.S. A resident alien gets a green card from the Immigration and Naturalization Service (INS).

Rights: Basic things we can do; our freedoms and privileges

PART ONE

U.S. GOVERNMENT STRUCTURE

LESSON 1

An Introduction to Government

OBJECTIVES
- Explain why we have governments
- Identify three levels of government

PRE-READING

Oral

Look at these pictures. Talk to your partner. Think of a word (or a few words) for each picture. Use these words:

world   **Mexico**   **federal**   **green card**

state   **citizen**   **local**

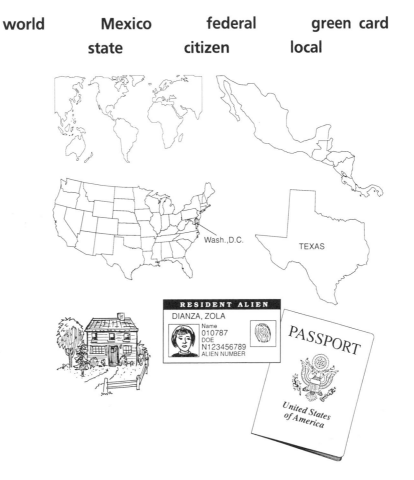

Vocabulary

Look at the words below on the left. They are important words. We will use these words many times in this book.

Read the sentences on the right. Can you find the word on the left in the sentence on the right? Circle the word.

government	The (government) makes laws for a country and helps the people.
federal	The national or federal government is for all of a country.
states	There are 50 states in the U.S.
local	I live in Texas. My city is Brownsville. Brownsville is my local area.
county	A county is a small part of a state. Miami is a city in Florida. Miami is in Dade County, Florida.
laws	Laws tell us things we can do and things we cannot do.

Map skills

Use maps of the world, the U.S., and your country.

1. Find the U.S.
2. Find your country.
3. Find your state in the U.S.
4. Find your state or province in your country.
5. Find your local area (city, county, town) in the U.S.
6. Find your local area in your country.

INFORMATION: Levels of Government

PLACE	LEVEL	WHAT IT DOES
Washington, D.C.	federal	makes laws for all of the country
Illinois	state	makes laws for one state
Chicago	local	makes laws for a small area in a state (city, county, etc.)

Using the Information

A. Look at the chart above. It has three columns. The first column gives you examples of different levels of government in the U.S.: Washington, D.C., Illinois, and Chicago.

   1. The second column lists the three levels of government.

      The levels are: _____, state, and local.

   2. The third column tells about the actions of the levels of government. Which level makes laws for all of the country?

   3. Which level makes laws for a small area?

B. Form a small group. Talk about U.S. laws you know. Make a list of some laws. Share your list with the other groups. Are U.S. laws the same or different from laws in other countries?

READING: Governments

The world is very big. There are many people in the world. There are many countries in the world. Every country has a government. The government makes the laws. The laws are for all the people in the country. The governments help people live together.

There are many different kinds of governments. In the U.S., we have a democracy. The citizens in a democracy choose people to be the leaders of the government by voting.

Using the Reading

C. Answer these questions:

   1. What does the government do?

   2. What kind of government do we have in the U.S.?

   3. What kind of government does your country have?

TESTING SKILLS

You will read many questions in exercises and on tests. Try to find the question word(s). This word helps you find the correct answer. For example, the question word **"who"** tells you to give a name.

Look at the questions below. Circle the question word. Write an answer.

1. Where do you live?

2. When did your family come to the U.S.?

3. How many states are in the U.S.?

You will see many **multiple choice** exercises in this book and on tests. First, read the question or top sentence. Then, read the choices below. One of the choices is the best. Circle the letter for the best answer.

EXAMPLE: How many levels of government do we have in the U.S.?

    a) one   **(b)** three   **c)** five

1. What level makes laws for all the country?
    a) local   **b)** state   **c)** federal

2. What level makes laws for a city?
    a) local   **b)** state   **c)** federal

3. What level makes laws for California?
    a) local   **b)** state   **c)** federal

REVIEW

What are the three levels of the U.S. government?

Why do we have governments?

LESSON 2

The Constitution: The Supreme Law of the Land

OBJECTIVES
- Explain the concept of a constitution
- Identify the three main principles of the Constitution

PRE-READING

Oral

Look at the chart below. It lists important ideas in the U.S. Constitution.

<u>1787</u>

"We the People"

supreme law of the land

self-government

basic rights

Discuss the following questions with the class.

1. Does your country or the country your family came from have a constitution?
2. How old is your constitution?
3. How old is the U.S. Constitution?
4. What ideas are in a constitution?

Written

Read the following sentences. Do you think they are true (**T**) or false (**F**)? Circle T or F.

1. The Constitution is very important in the U.S.   T   F
2. The Constitution tells us about basic rights.   T   F
3. The President makes all the laws in the U.S.   T   F
4. We write a new constitution every 100 years.   T   F

Vocabulary:

Use the following vocabulary words to finish the crossword puzzle. The meanings are at the top of page 9. You can use a dictionary to help you.

representative   supreme   government   guarantee
branch   protects   property   trial

ACROSS

2 Ruling a country by the people is self-__ __ __ __ __ __ __ __ __ __.

3 Defends = __ __ __ __ __ __ __ __.

6 The highest = __ __ __ __ __ __ __.

7 Someone acting in your place =
__ __ __ __ __ __ __ __ __ __ __ __.

DOWN

1 Part of the U.S. government = a __ __ __ __ __ __ of the U.S.
government

2 Promise = __ __ __ __ __ __ __ __ __ __.

4 Possession, something you own = __ __ __ __ __ __ __ __.

5 Legal action in court = __ __ __ __ __.

INFORMATION: Three Main Principles of the Constitution

1. BASIC RIGHTS	2. GOVERNMENT BY THE PEOPLE	3. SEPARATION OF POWERS
Freedom of speech Freedom of religion Right to have a trial Right to own property	People vote for their representatives People can ask for new laws or changes	Three branches of government with different powers

Using the Information

A. Complete the following paragraph. Use these words:

second	three	principles	religion
	basic	by	different

There are three main **1)** _principles_ of the U.S.

Constitution. The first one guarantees **2)** _____ rights. It

gives us freedom of speech and **3)** _____. The

4) _____ principle tells about a government **5)** _____

the people. The third principle tells about the **6)** _____

branches of the U.S. government. These branches have

7) _____ powers.

B. Form small groups. Talk about rules for your class. Which rules are very important? Talk about your rights as students. Write the important rules and rights as a group constitution. Share your constitution with the class. Try to write a class constitution together.

READING: The Supreme Law

The U.S. Constitution is the supreme law of the country. We cannot make any other laws against it. It tells us the important rules of our country. It protects the rights of <u>all</u> the people living in the U.S. Everyone must follow the Constitution or they can get into trouble. We have self-government in the federal, state, and local governments because we choose representatives. The representatives can make laws or change laws.

Using the Reading

C. Look again at the Reading above and the chart on page 7, then at the true and false questions on page 8. Can you answer them correctly now? Circle **T** or **F**.

1. The Constitution is very important in the U.S.	T	F
2. The Constitution tells us about basic rights.	T	F
3. The President makes all the laws in the U.S.	T	F
4. We write a new constitution every 100 years.	T	F

Here are some more true/false sentences:

5. We have self-government only at the federal level.	T	F
6. Some laws are more important than the Constitution.	T	F
7. Representatives can make changes in the laws.	T	F
8. The Constitution says that we can own property.	T	F

TESTING SKILLS

Sometimes the teacher asks you questions aloud. You have to listen very carefully. You should think about the question and then answer it.

You will see a set of two possible questions below. Your teacher will read one of those two questions. Listen carefully and read the choices. Which question did the teacher ask? Circle the letter of the correct question.

EXAMPLE: **a)** Who wrote the Constitution?
b) Who read the Constitution?

The teacher asks: *Who wrote the Constitution?* (listen)
You circle (a.)

1. a) Where did they write the Constitution?
   b) When did they write the Constitution?
2. a) How many main principles are in the Constitution?
   b) How many basic rights are in the Constitution?
3. a) Is self-government important to the American people?
   b) Is government by the people important?
4. a) In the Constitution, what are the three main branches?
   b) In the Constitution, why are there three main branches?
5. a) Do we have the right to a trial?
   b) Do we have the right to own property?

REVIEW

Do you know the three main principles? Can you explain them?

1) B __ __ I __ __ I __ __ T __

2) __ O __ __ __ N __ E __ __ __ Y T __ __   __ __ O P __ __

3) __ __ P __ __ A __ I __ __ O__ P __ __ E __ S

LESSON 3

The Constitution: The Preamble

OBJECTIVES | • Describe the structure of the Constitution
| • Identify the Preamble

PRE-READING

Oral

Discuss these questions with the class:

> You want to know about a TV show tonight. How can you find out about it?
>
> Suppose you want to go to a movie this weekend. There are two movies near your house. How can you find out about them?
>
> You go to the library. You want a book to read. How can you learn about the story before you read it?
>
> What is an introduction? Is it important? Why or why not?

Written

Read the following paragraph quickly to find the following words. Underline them.

welfare   justice   defense   establish

PREAMBLE

We the people of the United States, in order to form a more perfect Union, <u>establish</u> justice, insure domestic tranquility, provide for the common defense, promote the general welfare, and secure the blessings of liberty to ourselves and our posterity, do ordain and establish this Constitution for the United States of America.

Vocabulary

Match the words on the left with the meaning on the right. Put the correct letter on the line. You can use a dictionary to help you.

_C_	**1.** (to) **establish**	**a)** peace, calm, quiet
____	**2.** (to) **ordain**	**b)** doing well in life
____	**3. justice**	~~c)~~ to set up, to start
____	**4. domestic**	**d)** protection
____	**5. tranquility**	**e)** children, grandchildren, etc.
____	**6. posterity**	**f)** about the home or native land
____	**7. defense**	**g)** equal, fair action
____	**8. welfare**	**h)** good wishes
____	**9. blessings**	**i)** to order as a law

▉ INFORMATION: Parts of the Constitution ▉

PREAMBLE	=	Introduction
ARTICLES 1–7	=	Main points
AMENDMENTS	=	Additions and changes

PREAMBLE

You read the original Preamble in the beginning of the lesson. Here is another way to write the Preamble:

We are the people of the United States. We are writing this Constitution to have a better country. We want to set up a system of justice and to have peace in the country. We want to have an army to defend our country. We want to help people have a good life and to have liberty for ourselves and our children.

Using the Information

A. Check the sentences (✓) that tell about the Preamble:

____ **1.** It is the introduction of the Constitution.

____ **2.** It gives additions and changes to the Constitution.

____ **3.** It says the citizens want a better country.

____ **4.** It says the people do <u>not</u> want war in the country.

____ **5.** It says the people do <u>not</u> want an army to protect the country.

____ **6.** It says the people want freedom for their children.

B. Sometimes INS officials ask immigrants to read the Preamble. Look at the Preamble on page 12. Listen to your teacher read it aloud. Now you try. Read it to a partner.

TESTING SKILLS

Circle the letter of the <u>best</u> answer:

1. What section of the Constitution has seven parts?
   a) Preamble   **b)** Articles   **c)** Amendments

2. What section tells about the Constitution before you read it?
   a) Preamble   **b)** Articles   **c)** Amendments

3. Who is the Constitution for?
   a) citizens   **b)** resident aliens   **c)** all the people living in the U.S.

4. What does the Constitution help guarantee?
   a) liberty   **b)** war   **c)** money

REVIEW

List the parts of the Constitution.

The people of the United States wrote the Constitution for many reasons. Name three.

LESSON 4

The Constitution: The Articles

OBJECTIVE | • Identify the content of different articles in the Constitution

PRE-READING

Oral

Look at these pictures of important buildings. They have special meanings for Americans. Each building represents a branch of the federal government. Can you identify the buildings?

Many people work in these buildings.

1. Do you know any duties they have?

2. Do you think one branch has more power than the other two branches?

3. Do you have any contact with the federal government?

Vocabulary

Read the definitions below.

Legislative part of the government—the Congress (the House of Representatives + the Senate for the federal government)

Executive part of the government—the President, Vice President, and his helpers (or advisors) for the federal government

Judicial part of the government—the Supreme Court, other courts, and their judges

To **amend** the Constitution—to make some changes, to add some new things

To **ratify** the Constitution or an amendment—when three-fourths (3/4) of the states vote "yes"

Treaty—when the United States says it will do something or will not do something, together with another country. The President can suggest a treaty. The Senate must approve, or say "okay" to the treaty.

Written

Read the vocabulary. Circle the word that does <u>not</u> belong.

EXAMPLE: school   student   (car)   desk

ANSWER: car (because school, student, and desk are words about education)

1. Congress	Senate	Legislative	Preamble
2. Changes	Treaties	Additions	Amendments
3. Representatives	White House	Vice President	Executive
4. Judicial	Judges	Ratify	Courts

INFORMATION: Articles of the Constitution

The writers of the Constitution used Roman numerals for numbers.
I = 1, II = 2, III = 3, IV = 4, V = 5, VI = 6, VII = 7. The names
are the same: I = "one," V = "five."

ARTICLE	WHO	WHAT IT DOES
I	Legislative	• makes laws and decides taxes • okays treaties
II	Executive	• gives ideas for laws & treaties • is Chief of Army & Navy (President)
III	Judicial	• decides if laws are okay (judges) • helps protect people's rights
IV	States	• says all states have a republican form of government • tells each state to respect the laws of another state
V		• tells how to amend the Constitution
VI		• says the Constitution is the supreme law
VII		• tells how to ratify the Constitution

Using the Information

A. Look at the chart and vocabulary. Fill in the blanks.

1. There are ___seven___ articles in the Constitution.

2. Article I talks about the Congress or the House of

   _____ and the _____. They

   can _____ taxes and make new

   _____.

3. The President is the _____ of the army.

4. Information about the courts is in Article _____.

5. Article V says the government can change the Constitution.

   _____-fourths of the states must vote _____ to

   pass an amendment.

B. Work with a partner. One person reads the five sentences at the top of page 18. They are not true. The other person listens and makes them true.

1. The President okays treaties.
2. Article V tells us each state has a republican form of government.
3. The Senate decides if laws are okay.
4. Article IV tells about ratifying the Constitution.
5. The judicial part of the government decides taxes.

READING: The Articles of the Constitution

Article I. The Congress has many powers. It can decide taxes like the Social Security tax. It also makes laws about citizenship. Congress can start post offices, too. It makes laws about foreign trade. For example, if Honda, from Japan, wants to sell more cars in the U.S., the Congress decides yes or no. If the U.S. fights with another country, Congress can declare war.

Article II. The President has other powers. He or she is the Commander-in-Chief of the military. The President can choose people to be judges on the Supreme Court. He or she can choose people to be ambassadors. But, the Senate must say okay to these people. The President also gives information to the Congress. He or she tells Congress about problems in the U.S.

Article III. The Judicial branch has certain powers. The courts can review some laws. If the laws do not agree with the Constitution, the courts can tell Congress to change the laws. The courts listen to problems about protecting the Constitutional rights of the people.

Article IV. States have a republican form of government. States can make some state laws. All states must respect the laws of other states. If Congress says okay, new states can become part of the U.S.

Article V. This article explains the way to amend the Constitution. Three-fourths of the states must say okay to an amendment.

Article VI. This article says the Constitution is the supreme law of the U.S. Everyone must follow the Constitution.

Article VII. This article says three-fourths of the states must say okay to this Constitution. There were only 13 states in 1787.

Using the Reading

C. These sentences are about Articles I (legislative), II (executive), III (judicial), and IV (states). Put the number I, II, III, or IV next to the sentence that describes that Article.

    I   **1.** Tells about citizenship laws.

         2. Tells about protecting our rights.

____ **3.** Tells about choosing judges.

____ **4.** Tells about setting up places to mail letters and buy stamps.

____ **5.** Tells about setting up new states.

____ **6.** Tells about business with foreign countries.

____ **7.** Tells about the head of the army.

TESTING SKILLS

Read (or listen to) this conversation:

INS OFFICIAL: Okay, Mr. Mendoza. I will ask you some questions about the Constitution. Please tell me your answers.

MENDOZA: Okay.

INS OFFICIAL: In what year was the Constitution written?

MENDOZA: Written?

INS OFFICIAL: Yes, when did they write the Constitution?

MENDOZA: Let me think. . . . They wrote it in . . . in . . . in 1787.

INS OFFICIAL: Right. Let's continue. What are the three branches of government? . . .

Think about these questions:

1. Did Mr. Mendoza give his answer immediately?

2. Why did he say, "Written?"

3. Why did he repeat "in . . . in . . . "?

4. What do you say when you don't know the answer immediately?

5. Do you hear people say, "Let me think . . ."? Is this a good expression to use?

REVIEW

Do you know . . .

- how many articles are in the Constitution?
- which article talks about the executive branch?
- how we can change the Constitution?

LESSON 5 ═══════════════

The Constitution:
The Bill of Rights

OBJECTIVES
- Identify the Bill of Rights (Amendments 1–10)
- Show the importance of the Bill of Rights to all the people living in the U.S.

PRE-READING

Oral

Form a small group. Discuss the following situations. Record a group answer and share it with the class.

1. José wants to put a sign on his car, "VOTE for PABLO VELASQUEZ." Can he do this?
2. Carmen is a member of the Baptist Church. Is that okay in the U.S.?
3. The police stop Jean-Pierre. They take him to the station. Can he talk to a lawyer?
4. The police put Jean-Pierre in jail. He does not know why. He stays there for three years before he goes to trial. Is this okay in the U.S.?
5. A group of people in Arizona do not like a new law about buying guns. Can they tell the President they do not like the law? Can they write their opinion in the newspaper?

Vocabulary

Use the following words to complete the crossword puzzle. The definitions are below. You can use a dictionary to help you.

> unfair   accused   lawyer   fine   witnesses
> interfere   search   punishment   bail

ACROSS

3 <u>B A i L</u> — money you pay the court so you do not have to stay in jail while you wait for your day in court

6 ___ ___ ___ ___ ___ ___ ___ ___ ___ ___ — going to jail or paying a fine is an example of this

7 ___ ___ ___ ___ ___ ___ ___ ___ ___ ___ — people who speak in your favor or against you in court; they tell the court what they saw or what they know

8 ___ ___ ___ ___ ___ ___ — to look for something

9 ___ ___ ___ ___ ___ ___ ___ ___ ___ — to get in the way; to make problems

DOWN

1 ___ ___ ___ ___ — the money you must pay because you did something wrong

2 ___ ___ ___ ___ ___ ___ — not appropriate; too much or too little

4 ___ ___ ___ ___ ___ ___ ___ — when someone says you did something wrong

5 ___ ___ ___ ___ ___ ___ ___ — a person who studies the laws and court systems; he/she can help you in court or with other problems

READING: Freedom

Freedom is the most important right we have in the U.S. In the 1600's, people came to find freedom. What is freedom?

Freedom means you can. . .

- follow any religion
- say and write your ideas
- choose your type of work
- have meetings when you want
- live where you want

- ask the government to make changes
- live in peace

The U.S. Constitution and the U.S. government protect the rights and freedom of all the people living in the U.S. No one can **interfere** with the rights of other people. No one can take away your rights if you follow the law. We should all follow the laws and protect everyone's rights.

Using the Reading

A. Form a small group. Read and discuss the following sentence. What do you think it means? Share your group's ideas with the class.

"My freedom ends where your freedom begins."

INFORMATION: The Bill of Rights (Amendments 1–10)

Amendment 1. Freedom of Religion, Speech, the Press, and Assembly

> We can follow any religion; we can say our thoughts; we can write articles in newspapers; we can meet in groups.

Amendment 2. The Right to Have Guns

> We can have guns for protection. State governments make laws about buying and keeping guns.

Amendment 3. Housing Soldiers

> We do not have to let soldiers stay in our homes in peace time. If there is a war, Congress can pass a law to let soldiers stay in our homes.

Amendment 4. Searches and Warrants

> Police need a court order (search warrant) to search our homes or to take our things.

Amendment 5. Rights of People Accused of a Crime, and Protection of Private Property

> If a judge says you are free at a trial, you do not go to a second trial for the same crime.
> You do not have to answer questions at your trial.
> The government must pay a fair price before taking private property from someone.

Amendment 6. Right to a Fair Trial and Witnesses

> If you are accused of a crime, you have the right to know why.
> You have the right to a speedy and public trial with a jury.
> You have the trial in the state where the crime happened.
> You can have a private lawyer or the court will give you a lawyer.
> The lawyers can question all the witnesses.
> You can have witnesses on your side.

Amendment 7. Right to a Jury Trial

> If the money in your case is over twenty dollars ($20.00), you can have a jury trial.

Amendment 8. Bails, Fines, and Punishments

> A judge cannot make you pay an unfair bail. A judge or jury cannot make you pay an unfair fine. A judge or jury or the police cannot give you unfair punishment.

Amendment 9. The People Keep Some Rights

> The Constitution lists many rights of the people, but it does not list all the rights. The people have other rights, too.

Amendment 10. The States or People Keep Some Powers

> The Constitution lists some powers for the federal government, but it cannot list all the powers. The other powers are for the states or for the people.

Using the Information

B. Read the following sentences about rights. Which amendment gives you each right? Put the number of the amendment next to the sentence about it.

a) __4__ A policeman shows you a court order and he comes into your apartment.

b) _____ A TV newswoman does not like a treaty the President made with China. On TV, she says the treaty is bad.

c) _____ The people have some rights that are not written in the Constitution.

d) _____ You must complete an application form and wait 7 days if you want to buy a gun in the state of Maryland.

e) _____ A poor man does not have money for a lawyer. The court gives him a lawyer.

f) _____ The police must tell you why they are taking you to the police station.

g) _____ The court says you are wrong. You must go to jail for 5 years.

C. Work with a partner. Discuss these questions. Share your answers with the class.

1. Does your country have jury trials?
2. Does your country put people in jail without trials?
3. Do the people have freedom of speech in your country?
4. Can you name a country without religious freedom?
5. Do you think the Bill of Rights is important? Why or why not?

TESTING SKILLS

Complete the following sentences.

1. The First Amendment gives us freedom of _____, _____, and _____.

2. The police need a _____ before they can search our homes.

3. If the police take you to the police station, you have the right to talk to a _____.

4. We have the right to a _____ and _____ trial with a jury.

5. A judge cannot give you an unfair _____.

REVIEW

The First Amendment guarantees some basic rights. Name two.

Some amendments help people accused of crimes. Name one.

LESSON 6

The Constitution: Amendments 11–26

OBJECTIVES

- Identify Amendments 11–26
- Discuss the importance of the amendment process

PRE-READING

Oral

Look at the following pictures. What is happening? Does the Constitution discuss these situations?

Vocabulary

Use a dictionary. Find the meaning of these words.

slavery—

26

(to) **repeal**—

(to) **resign** (from a job)—

restrictions—

Written

Scanning is an important reading skill. Scanning = reading quickly to find information. Read the questions below. Then look at the Information. Scan it to find the answers. Circle **Y** (Yes) or **N** (No).

EXAMPLE: Look at Amendment 13.

Can we have slavery in the U.S.?   Y   Ⓝ

1. Look at Amendment 15. Can Black people
vote?   Y   N

2. Do some of the amendments tell us who can
vote?   Y   N

3. Do some of the amendments discuss electing a
President?   Y   N

4. Do some of the amendments discuss taxes?   Y   N

INFORMATION: Amendments 11–26

Amendment 11. Citizens of one state or a foreign country cannot bring a case against another state in a federal court.

Amendment 12. We elect the President and Vice President separately.

Amendment 13. There is no more slavery in the U.S.

Amendment 14. All people born or naturalized in the U.S. are citizens.

Amendment 15. Black people have the right to vote.

Amendment 16. Congress can make a law for an income tax.

Amendment 17. We elect Senators directly with our votes.

Amendment 18. It is illegal to make or sell liquor in the U.S.

Amendment 19. Women have the right to vote.

Amendment 20. A new President takes office on January 20.

Amendment 21. This repeals the 18th Amendment. Now it is legal to make or sell liquor in the U.S.

Amendment 22. We can elect the same President for two terms. Each term is for 4 years.

Amendment 23. Citizens of Washington, DC, can vote for President and Vice President.

Amendment 24. We do not have to pay a voting tax.

Amendment 25. If the President dies or resigns, the Vice President becomes President. This amendment also tells the order for other important government officials to become President if something happens to the Vice President, etc.

Amendment 26. Citizens 18 years old or older can vote.

Using the Information

A. Form a small group. Discuss the following pictures. Do the pictures tell us anything about Amendments 11–26?

B. Organize Amendments 11–26 into the following categories. List the numbers of the amendments:

VOTING / ELECTIONS	FREEDOMS / RESTRICTIONS
a) ___	j) ___
b) ___	k) ___
c) ___	l) ___
d) ___	m) ___
e) ___	**INCOME TAX**
f) ___	n) ___
g) ___	**CASES IN FEDERAL COURT**
h) ___	o) ___
PRESIDENT ENTERS OFFICE	**IF PRESIDENT DIES OR RESIGNS**
i) ___	p) ___

READING: The Amendment Process

We have a *living* Constitution. Men wrote it in 1787, and we still use it today. These men were intelligent. "The U.S. will change in the future," they thought. "We must find a way to let the Constitution change too." And they did.

They put in the amendment process. This process is important. Amendments can change or add rights and restrictions to the Constitution. An amendment can change part of an article in the Constitution or another amendment.

Two-thirds (2/3) of the Congress or of the state legislatures must agree on an idea for an amendment. If three-fourths (3/4) of the states ratify the amendment, it becomes part of the Constitution.

Using the Reading

C. Write questions using these words. Answer your questions. The first one is done for you as an example.

1. How / change / Constitution?
   Q: How can we change the Constitution?
   A: By amendment.

2. Who / must agree / idea / amendment?

3. How many / states / ratify / amendment?

4. Why / we / amend / Constitution?

TESTING SKILLS

With multiple choice tests, you can learn to make good guesses. One or two of the choices are always wrong. Look at the questions below. Look carefully at the question word. There are three possible answers. One answer is clearly wrong. Think carefully and put an **X** on that answer. You do <u>not</u> have to find the right answer.

EXAMPLE: What do we call changes to the Constitution?

      a) articles   ~~**b)**~~ men in Congress   **c)** amendments

One clearly wrong answer is **(b)** because it answers the question "Who?", not the question "What?"

1. How many members of Congress must approve an idea for an amendment?
   a) three-fourths   **b)** two-thirds   **c)** the state legislatures

2. According to Amendment 16, what can Congress tax?
   a) every 4 years   **b)** income   **c)** liquor

3. Who can vote for President?
   a) women   **b)** for two terms   **c)** a 16-year-old man

4. When did they write the Constitution?
   a) to put in the amendment process
   b) in 1887
   c) over 200 years ago

REVIEW

Can citizens over 18 years old vote?	Y	N
Can Blacks vote?	Y	N
Can a President be elected for four terms?	Y	N
Can we buy and sell liquor?	Y	N
The President dies. Does your Senator to Congress become President?	Y	N

LESSON 7

Review: The Constitution

This lesson will help you review the information in Lessons 1–7. If you need help with these exercises, you can look back at these lessons.

A. Complete the following crossword puzzle.

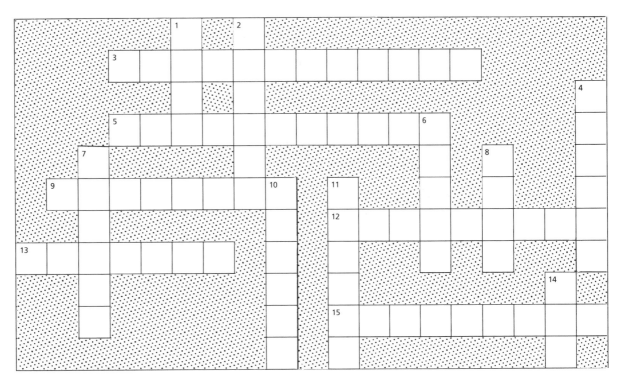

ACROSS

3 The first ten amendments (three words).
5 Congress is in the _____ branch.
9 Senate + House of Representatives = _____.
12 The President is head of the _____ branch.
13 The first amendment guarantees _____ of press and religion.
15 An addition to the U.S. Constitution.

DOWN

1 Symbol for the U.S. It is red, white, and blue.
2 There are two _____: the White _____ and the _____ of Representatives.
4 If you go to court, a _____ can help you.
6 We _____ a President every 4 years.
7 Separation of _____.
8 The 19th amendment says women can _____.
10 The 1st amendment gives us freedom of _____. We can say our thoughts.
11 To take back; the 21st amendment __ __ __ __ __ __ E D the 18th amendment.
14 How many U.S. Supreme Courts are in the U.S. government?

B. Read the following groups of sentences. One sentence is false in each group. Circle the letter of the false one.

1. a) We have four levels of government in the U.S.: international, federal, state, and local.

   b) The Constitution is for all people in the U.S.

   c) We have a democracy in the U.S.

2. a) The U.S. Constitution is over 300 years old.

   b) Separation of powers is one of the three main principles of the Constitution.

   c) A constitution gives a plan to rule a country.

3. a) The Preamble is an introduction to the Constitution.

   b) The writers of the Constitution wanted peace in the country.

   c) The Constitution says the U.S. cannot fight in a war.

4. a) There are three branches in the U.S. government.

   b) Article I says the executive makes the laws.

   c) Article V discusses the amendment process.

5. a) The Bill of Rights is the first five amendments of the Constitution.

   b) The Bill of Rights gives us freedom of speech and religion.

   c) The Bill of Rights gives us the right to a trial.

6. a) in 1987, the Constitution had 26 amendments.

   b) The amendments give black people, women, and people over 16 years old the right to vote.

   c) Some amendments discuss elections.

C. Now write those six false sentences. Make them true.

1) _____

_____

2) _____

_____

3) _____

_____

4) _____

_____

5) _____

_____

6) _____

_____

D. Match the information on the left with its location in the Constitution. Put the correct letter on the line.

_____ **1.** We have the right to a lawyer.

_____ **2.** Congress passes laws.

_____ **3.** Three-fourths of the states must approve an amendment.

_____ **4.** We can elect a President for only two terms.

_____ **5.** We have the right to say our thoughts.

_____ **6.** The President is Chief of the Army and Navy.

_____ **7.** The Judicial Branch decides if laws are okay.

_____ **8.** We want liberty for ourselves and our children.

a) Preamble
b) Article I
c) Article II
d) Article III
e) Article V
f) Amendment 1
g) Amendment 6
h) Amendment 22

E. Look at these pictures again. What does the Constitution tell us about them? Share your ideas with the class.

LESSON 8

Executive Branch: President and Vice President

OBJECTIVES | • Identify the powers of the executive branch
• Identify the qualifications of the President and Vice President

PRE-READING

Oral

Discuss these questions with the class:

Who is the President of the U.S.?

Who is the Vice President of the U.S.?

Tell the class about the leader of your country:

Is your leader a "president"?

If not, what do you call your leader?

What is the leader's name?

Can all adult citizens vote for the leader?

Listen to your classmates. Put the information about their countries in the chart below:

COUNTRY	LEADER	NAME	ADULTS CAN VOTE	
			YES	NO
U.S.A.	President		✓	

Can you name the pictures of two famous Presidents? Do you know anything about these U.S. Presidents?

Vocabulary

Read the following definitions.

V.P.—Vice President

(to) **veto**—to say "no"

(to) **approve**—to say "yes" or "okay"

(to) **appoint**—to choose

(to) **advise**—to give help and information

(to) **pardon**—to forgive a person for a federal crime; to give amnesty

soldiers—people in the Army, Navy, and Air Force

U.S. **foreign policy**—the way the U.S. government plans to act with other countries of the world

Written

Use the vocabulary above to unscramble the following words:

1. tevo _____

3. savedi _____

2. paveorp _____

4. toppina _____

Put three of these four words into the following sentences.

1. The Senate can _____ treaties.

2. The President needs help. The Vice President can _____ her or him.

3. I want to be a judge. Do you think the President will

_____ me?

INFORMATION: Duties of the President and Vice President

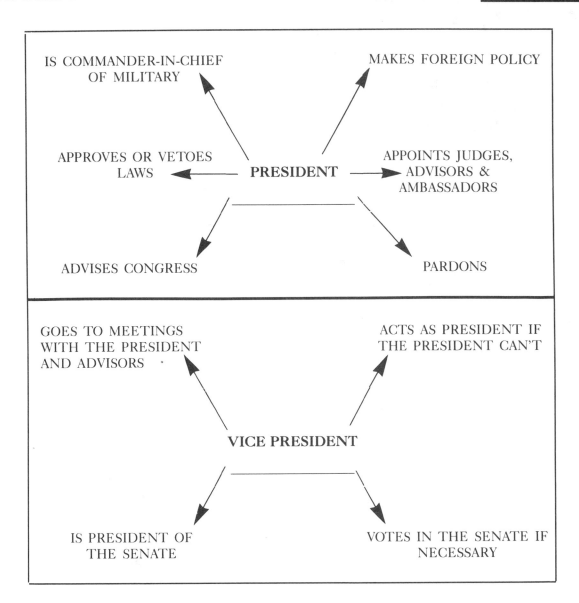

Using the Information

A. Look at the vocabulary and the information above. Read the following sentences. The President can do three of these things. Check the three correct sentences.

The President . . .

_____ **1.** makes plans for foreign policy.

_____ **2.** appoints people to the Supreme Court.

_____ **3.** writes taxes for states.

_____ **4.** votes in the Senate.

_____ **5.** sends soldiers to war.

B. Form a small group. Talk about the activities of the President and the V.P. of the U.S.

What did they do this past week?

Did they go to another state or country?

Did they meet important people?

Make a list of all the things you remember. Share the information with the class.

READING: Qualifications of the President and Vice President

Do you want to be President? You must be born in the United States. You must live in the U.S. for 14 years or more. You must also be 35 years old or more. You can be President for a term of 4 years. You can be elected again for one more term.

If the President dies, or resigns, or can't work, the Vice President becomes President. So, the qualifications for Vice President are the same as for the President.

Using the Reading

C. Look at the Reading. The lists below show the qualifications for President and Vice President. Fill in the missing information.

PRESIDENT

1) __35__ + years old

2) be born _____

3) live in the U.S. for ____ years

4) only ____ elected terms

VICE PRESIDENT

5) ____ + years old

6) be born _____

7) live in the U.S. for ____ years

TESTING SKILLS

Circle the letter of the best answer.

1. Who is President of the Senate?
   a) the Vice President   **b)** a representative   **c)** a judge

2. A president does not like an idea for a new tax law. The president can _____ it.
   a) appoint   **b)** pardon   **c)** veto

3. Which one can a President *not* appoint?
   a) a judge   **b)** a senator   **c)** an ambassador

4. Can someone be President for 16 years?
   a) yes   **b)** no
5. Someone is 30 years old. Can this person be Vice President?
   a) yes   **b)** no

REVIEW

Can you answer these questions?

1. Who is the President of the U.S.?
2. Who is the Vice President?
3. What are three things a President can do?
4. What is one thing a Vice President can do?
5. Why do we have a Vice President?

LESSON 9

Executive Branch: The Cabinet

OBJECTIVES
- Explain the role of the Cabinet
- Match executive departments with their responsibilities

PRE-READING

Oral

Look at the sequence of pictures. What do you think is happening?

Written

Read the following sentences. Each sentence tells about one of the pictures on page 40. Put the number of the picture next to the correct sentence.

_____ **a)** The President meets with the Cabinet. They talk about a problem. The Cabinet gives advice to the President.

_____ **b)** The President listens to Cabinet members with different ideas. One wants to build new apartments. The other member says it is too expensive.

_____ **c)** The President makes a decision and the Cabinet members agree.

_____ **d)** The President thinks about the problem.

Vocabulary

Read the following definitions.

The **Cabinet** is a group of advisors to the President. They are in charge of the executive departments.

We call most Cabinet members **"Secretary."** For example, Thomas Jefferson was the first Secretary of State. The State Department advises the President about foreign policy.

The head of the Justice Department is the **Attorney General.**

A **veteran** was a soldier.

Juan needs money for college. He asks for **financial aid.**

Hilda is looking for some information. She goes to the library to do some **research.**

It is a very hot summer. We need to save water. We practice water **conservation.** We use water carefully.

We must get a car **inspection** every year. We take our cars to a service station. A mechanic checks the car. He looks at the lights, brakes, and tires.

INFORMATION: The Cabinet

| STATE
• foreign policy
• treaties | TREASURY
• tax collection
• money | DEFENSE
• military advice
• Army, Navy, Air Force |

| VETERANS AFFAIRS
• financial aid
• VA hospitals | JUSTICE
• legal advice
• INS | INTERIOR
• National Parks
• American Indians |

| AGRICULTURE
• farming
• food inspection | COMMERCE
• business
• trade | LABOR
• rights of workers
• job training |

| HEALTH & HUMAN SERVICES
• health services
• social security | HOUSING & URBAN DEVELOPMENT
• housing
• city planning |

| TRANSPORTATION
• travel safety
• road, air, and train travel | EDUCATION
• schools
• financial aid | ENERGY
• energy research
• energy conservation |

Using the Information

A. Match the Cabinet department on the left with its responsibility on the right. Put the correct letter on the line.

_____ **1.** Education

_____ **2.** Health & Human Services

_____ **3.** Treasury

_____ **4.** Justice

a) takes tax money from our paychecks

b) helps train people for employment

c) plans for special classes

_____ **5.** Labor

_____ **6.** Housing & Urban Development

d) helps build low-cost housing
e) gives green cards
f) gives Social Security cards

B. Listen to your teacher explain the game "Who Am I?" One student is a Cabinet member. The other students ask "yes/no" questions about his/her responsibilities. Try to guess the Cabinet member.

EXAMPLE: Do you help farmers?

READING: The Cabinet and the President

There are 14 executive departments. The heads of the executive departments are Cabinet members. The President appoints the members to the Cabinet. The President has weekly meetings with the Cabinet. They discuss problems. The Cabinet members advise the President.

Using the Reading

C. Read the following answers. Write a question for the answer. Use the information in the reading above.

EXAMPLE: Question— _Who advises the President_ ?

Answer— Cabinet members

1) _____ ?
   14

2) _____ ?
   The President

3) _____ ?
   problems

TESTING SKILLS

Read the following conversation. Circle the letter of the best answer for Ms. Abdul.

QUESTIONER: Okay, we know the President and the Vice President are part of the executive branch. Is there anyone else?

Ms. Abdul: **1. a)** No, there is not.
      b) Yes, the Congress.
      c) Yes, the Cabinet.

Questioner: What is the role of the Cabinet?

Ms. Abdul: **2. a)** The role. . .?
      b) I don't know the Cabinet.
      c) You tell me.

Questioner: The responsibilities.

Ms. Abdul: **3. a)** No.
      b) Let me think. . . .
      c) Yes, they have.

Questioner: Can you tell me one responsibility?

Ms. Abdul: **4. a)** They have many.
      b) Ahh . . . the Cabinet appoints the President.
      c) Well, I think the Cabinet advises the President.

REVIEW

What is the Cabinet?

Name three executive (or Cabinet) departments.

LESSON 10

Executive Branch: Independent Agencies

OBJECTIVE | • Identify one independent agency

PRE-READING

Oral

Look at the four pictures. Talk about the pictures with your partner. What is the relationship between the pictures and the U.S. Government?

Vocabulary

Read the following words and their definitions.

agency—an office of the U.S. Government

discrimination—to say "no" to someone because of race, age, sex, religion, etc.

pollution—dirt in the air, in the water, on the ground, etc.

INFORMATION: Independent Agencies

There are many independent agencies in the executive branch. They are independent because they are not part of any executive department. Some agencies and their responsibilities are:

AGENCY	RESPONSIBILITY
Environmental Protection Agency (EPA)	helps stop pollution
National Aeronautic and Space Administration (NASA)	plans the space program
U.S. Postal Service	delivers mail
Commission on Civil Rights	helps stop discrimination

Using the Information

Look at the chart and read the following stories. Which agency should help these people? Discuss the stories with a partner.

1. Kim always likes to go fishing on Sunday. Last week he went to the river near his house. He saw a lot of dead fish in the river.

   AGENCY: _____

2. Anna's parents live far away. She does not see them very often. She likes to send them letters.

   AGENCY: _____

3. Juliana is from Puerto Rico. She finished high school in New York last year. She applied for a job yesterday. The manager said he wanted a man for the job.

   AGENCY: _____

REVIEW

Some government agencies, like the EPA, can help you. Name another agency.

LESSON 11

The Election Process

OBJECTIVE | • Explain the election process

PRE-READING

Oral

Look at the picture below. Some of these people are waiting to vote.

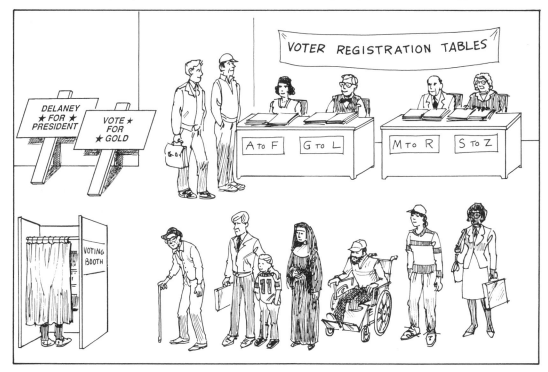

Discuss these questions with your partner:

1. Do you think all the people in the picture will vote? Why or why not?

2. Will they vote for President or Senator?

3. Can you vote? Why or why not?

4. How do people vote in your country?

Vocabulary

Use the dictionary to find definitions for these words. Write a short definition.

ballot – a paper used for voting

campaign

candidate

election

elector

inauguration

primary

INFORMATION: The Election Process for President

A **political party** is a group of people with the same ideas about government. There are two main political parties in the U.S.: the **Republican Party** and the **Democratic Party**. Also, there are many other smaller parties.

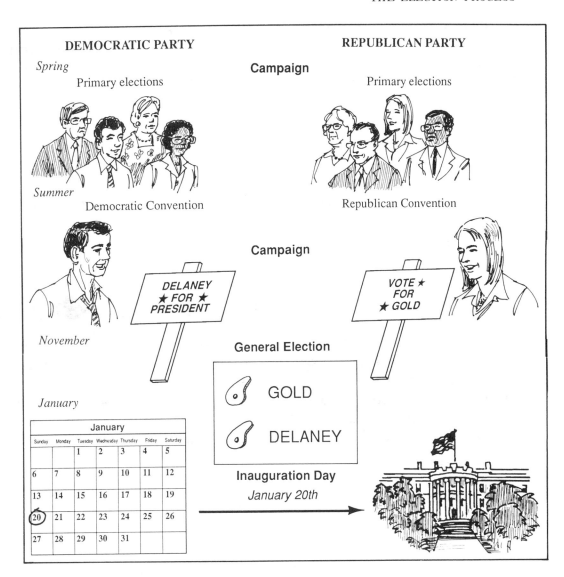

Using the Information

A. Read the following sentences. They tell about the election process. They are in the wrong order. Put the numbers 1–5 on the lines to show the correct order.

_____ **a)** U.S. adult citizens vote for a President in a national election.

_____ **b)** At first, there are two or more candidates for the Republican Party and two or more candidates for the Democratic Party.

_____ **c)** After the party conventions, the candidates continue to campaign.

_____ **d)** The inauguration of the President is on January 20th.

_____ **e)** In the summer, each party has a convention to choose one candidate.

B. Have a class discussion about elections. Talk about the process in the U.S. and in your country. Here are some questions to help you.

1. How many political parties are in your country?
2. Who can vote in your country?
3. How do people vote in your country?
4. How often do you have elections?
5. Does the law say, "All adult citizens must vote"?
6. Is there a fine or punishment if you do not vote?
7. Is the election process in your country the same as in the U.S.?

READING: The Electoral College

When the citizens vote for the President, they are really voting for state **electors**. These electors form the Electoral College. Every state has electors. The number of electors equals the number of senators + the number of representatives in a state. For example, Alaska has two senators and one representative. So, Alaska has three electors. Florida has two senators and 19 representatives. So Florida has 21 electors.

This is what happens:

1. Citizens of a state vote.
2. Their votes are counted.
3. One candidate has 51% or more of the votes.
4. This candidate wins all the electoral votes of that state.
5. The electoral votes of all the states are counted.
6. The candidate with the most electoral votes becomes the President.

Using the Reading

C. Look at the following information about the state of New Jersey. Answer the questions. Write the numbers on the line.

2 senators + 14 representatives = _____ electors

60% vote for Mr. Angeli
28% vote for Ms. Parson
12% vote for Mr. Roth

1. How many electoral votes will Mr. Angeli win? _____

2. How many electoral votes will Ms. Parson win? _____

3. How many electoral votes will Mr. Roth win? _____

TESTING SKILLS

Read the first sentence. Circle the letter of the other sentence with the same meaning.

1. All adult citizens of the U.S. can vote in a national election.
   a) All citizens must vote.
   b) All citizens have the right to vote.
   c) All citizens want to vote.

2. In an election year, candidates make many campaign speeches.
   a) Candidates make speeches only at the convention.
   b) Candidates make speeches at the inauguration.
   c) Candidates make speeches during the election process.

3. There are many political parties in the U.S.
   a) There are two main political parties.
   b) There are the Republican, Democratic, and other political parties.
   c) The largest parties are the Republican and the Democratic parties.

REVIEW

Can you explain the election process? Use these words to help you.

primary elections   campaigns   summer conventions   election day

LESSON 12

Legislative Branch: Congress

OBJECTIVES
- Identify the two parts of Congress
- State the responsibilities of Congress

PRE-READING

Oral

Look at the picture of the U.S. Capitol in Washington, D.C.

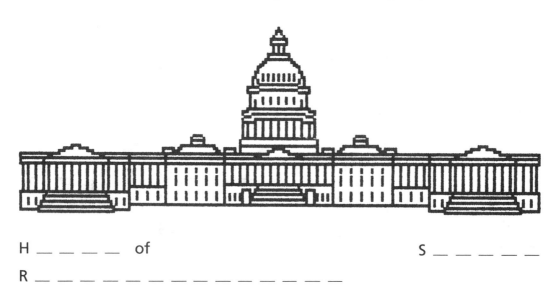

H _ _ _ _ of   S _ _ _ _ _

R _ _ _ _ _ _ _ _ _ _ _ _ _ _

Discuss these questions with your partner.

1. What city is the capital of the U.S.?
2. What is the capital of your country?
3. The U.S. Congress has two parts. What do we call them?
4. Does your country have a Congress?

52

Vocabulary

Read the following definitions.

(to) declare war—to tell the people "our country will fight"

authorization—legal permission or okay

title of nobility—an upper-class name ("king," "queen," "lord," etc.)

(to) maintain—to support with money

exports—things the U.S. sells to other countries

Written

Scan the sentences below. Then look at the following chart. Find the answers quickly. Circle **Y** (yes) or **N** (no).

1. Congress can declare war.	Y	N
2. Congress can give a title of nobility.	Y	N
3. Congress can maintain an army.	Y	N
4. Congress can make laws about marriage.	Y	N

INFORMATION: Duties of the Congress

The Constitution lists some duties for both the House of Representatives and the Senate. The Constitution also lists some things Congress cannot do. Read the chart below.

CONGRESS CAN . . .	CONGRESS CANNOT . . .
• make laws about trade • maintain Army, Navy, Air Force • declare war • make laws about taxes • make laws about citizenship • establish U.S. Post Office • make laws about the District of Columbia • borrow money • print money	• put a tax on exports • give title of nobility • use tax money without authorization • take away the right to a trial • make laws about marriage, driver's licenses, police, etc. (These are done by the states.)

Using the Information

A. Read the following sentences. Write "yes" next to the sentences about things Congress can do. Write "no" next to the sentences about things Congress cannot do.

———— **1.** say a person cannot have a trial in court

———— **2.** make new laws

———— **3.** send the army to war

———— **4.** say if a person can be a citizen

———— **5.** put a tax on things the U.S. sells to other countries

———— **6.** say a person is the King of America

———— **7.** maintain a police force

B. Form a small group. The Constitution lists some things Congress cannot do. The writers of the Constitution had a reason for this list. What do you think the reasons are? Discuss them with your group. Write your answers and share them with the class.

EXAMPLE: Congress cannot give titles of nobility. Why not?

Because the writers wanted all Americans to be equal. They did not want anyone to become king or queen.

1. Congress cannot take away the right to a trial. Why not?

2. Congress cannot make laws about marriage. Why not?

3. Congress cannot use tax money without authorization. Why not?

READING: The Congress

Read the following paragraph from the *Federal Citizenship Text—U. S. Government Structure:*

"The Constitution established that the Congress must meet regularly. A new Congress begins every two years, with the election of new Senators and Representatives. The time they meet to make laws is called a **session**. Congress meets in the Capitol Building in Washington, D.C. The House of Representatives has a large room, the Senate a smaller one, and the President has some offices for his/her use."

Using the Reading

C. Use the words below to write questions. Then answer the questions.

    1. When / new Congress / begin?

_____ ?

_____ .

    2. What / we call / meeting / Congress?

_____ ?

_____ .

    3. Where / Congress / meet?

_____ ?

_____ .

TESTING SKILLS

Read (or listen to) the conversation.

    INS OFFICIAL: What are the three branches of the U.S. government?

    MS. YANG: Three branches . . . one is executive, one is judicial, and . . . and . . . and the last one is legislative.

    INS OFFICIAL: Tell me a little about the legislative branch.

    MS. YANG: I'm not sure. I don't understand the question. Do you mean . . . I should talk about Congress?

    INS OFFICIAL: Yes. What can you tell me about the U.S. Congress?

    MS. YANG: Okay. The Congress has two parts: the

_____ and the

_____ .

Think about these questions:

    1. Did Ms. Yang give all the answers immediately?

    2. Why did she say, "Do you mean . . . I should talk about Congress?"

    3. What can you say if you do not understand a question?

    4. Can you finish the last line for Ms. Yang?

REVIEW

Can you name . . .

- two things Congress can do?

- two things Congress cannot do?

LESSON 13

Legislative Branch:
The House of Representatives

OBJECTIVES | • Explain duties of the House of Representatives
| • Identify the qualifications of a representative

PRE-READING

Oral

Look at the map of the U.S. The map shows you the number of representatives for some states.

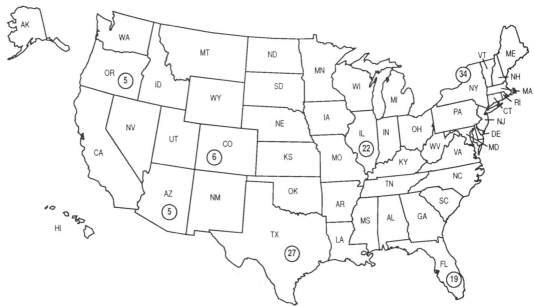

Discuss these questions with your partner.

1. Does every state have the same number of representatives?

2. How many representatives does your state have?

3. Do you know the names of your representatives? Where can you find their names?

4. Does your country have representatives? How many?

Vocabulary

Complete the crossword puzzle. Use these words:

House	**impeach**	**district**	**Representative**
represent	**officials**	**budget**	**bill** **propose**

ACROSS

2 A member of the House of Representatives is a
___ ___ ___ ___ ___ ___ ___ ___ ___ ___ ___ ___ ___ ___.

5 A short form for House of Representatives is to say the
___ ___ ___ ___ ___.

6 An idea for a new law is a ___ ___ ___ ___.

7 The voters elect officials. The officials ___ ___ ___ ___ ___ ___ ___ ___ ___
the people.

8 If an official does something unconstitutional, the House can
___ ___ ___ ___ ___ ___ ___ the official. The House tells the country the
official did something wrong.

DOWN

1 People with important jobs in the government are called
___ ___ ___ ___ ___ ___ ___ ___.

3 To give an idea for the first time or to suggest an idea is to
___ ___ ___ ___ ___ ___ ___ an idea.

4 An area in a city or state is a ___ ___ ___ ___ ___ ___ ___ ___.

6 A plan for spending money is a ___ ___ ___ ___ ___ ___.

▮ INFORMATION: Members of the House of Representatives ▮

There are 435 members in the House of Representatives.

QUALIFICATIONS	REPRESENTS	SPECIAL DUTIES
Age: 25+ years U.S. Citizen: 7+ years Live: in state Term: 2 years Limit: none	IOWA • Des Moines 1 district	• impeach officials • propose bills on budget or taxes

Using the Information

A. Choose a partner. Student A reads sentences 1–3. Every sentence has a mistake in it. Student B looks at the chart and tries to repeat the sentence with the correct information. Switch roles for sentences 4–6. Student B reads and Student A corrects.

EXAMPLE: **A)** A representative must be 35 or older.

B) No. A representative must be 25 or older.

1. **A)** A representative represents two states.

   B) _____

2. **A)** There are 455 members in the House.

   B) _____

3. **A)** Only the Senate can propose tax bills.

   B) _____

4. **B)** The term for a representative is 4 years.

   A) _____

5. **B)** Representatives must be citizens for 14 years.

   A) _____

6. **B)** Representatives can appoint officials.

   A) _____

B. Now read the same sentences again. Circle the mistake. Write the correction under the circled mistake.

EXAMPLE: **1. A)** A representative represents (two states.)

   B) A representative represents one district.

READING: The Number of Representatives

There are 435 Representatives in the House. States with large populations have many representatives. In the 1980's, there was usually one representative for about every 580,000 people in a state. However, all states must have at least one representative. For example, Idaho has a population of 998,000. Idaho has two representatives. But, Alaska has only 525,000 people. Alaska has one representative. States with many representatives have more power in the House than states with only a few representatives.

Some states have many districts. The number of districts is equal to the number of representatives. The citizens of a district vote directly for their representative. Representatives listen to the needs of the people in their districts and their states.

Using the Reading

C. Look at the maps of five different states. The number below the map tells us the population of that state in 1987. How many representatives did each state have? Write the number on the line below the population. Use these numbers:

1   2   10   11   45

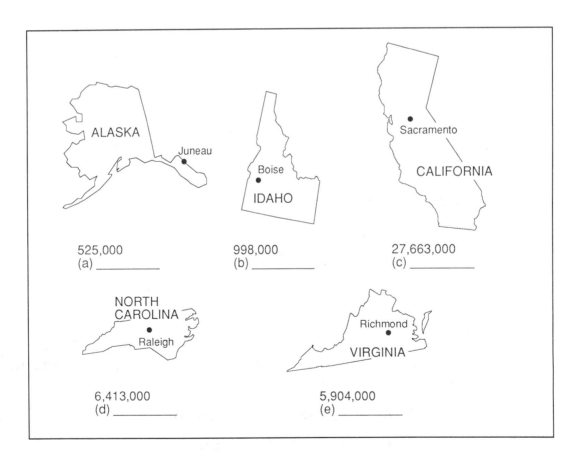

ALASKA
Juneau

Boise
IDAHO

Sacramento
CALIFORNIA

525,000
(a) _____

998,000
(b) _____

27,663,000
(c) _____

NORTH CAROLINA
Raleigh

Richmond
VIRGINIA

6,413,000
(d) _____

5,904,000
(e) _____

TESTING SKILLS

Circle the letter of the best answer.

1. There are _____ members in the House of Representatives.
   a) 100   **b)** 534   **c)** 435

2. A representative must be a citizen for _____ years before election.
   a) 9   **b)** 7   **c)** 14

3. Every state has at least _____ representative(s).
   a) one   **b)** two   **c)** three

4. Only the House can _____ officials.
   a) tax   **b)** count   **c)** impeach

5. Each representative represents _____.
   a) two states   **b)** two or three districts   **c)** one district

REVIEW

Do you know . . .

- one duty of the House of Representatives?
- two qualifications of a representative?
- the number of representatives for your state?
- the name of your representative?

LESSON 14

Legislative Branch: The Senate

OBJECTIVES
- Explain the duties of the Senate
- Identify the qualifications of a senator

PRE-READING

Oral

Look at the map of the U.S. Every state has two senators.

Work with a partner. Discuss these questions.

1. How many senators work in the U.S. Congress?
2. Does every state have equal power in the Senate?
3. Who is the president of the Senate?

4. Do you know the names of your U.S. senators? Where can you find their names?

5. Does your or your family's country have senators? How many?

Vocabulary

Read the following definitions.

(to) **try** a public official—The Senate will decide if an official really did something unconstitutional (against the Constitution).

(to) **remove** from office—to tell an official to leave his/her job.

(to) **confirm appointments**—to approve people the President chooses for judges, ambassadors, and cabinet members.

majority—more than half; 51% or more.

Written

Read the vocabulary. Circle the word that does <u>not</u> belong.

EXAMPLE: House   Senate   Congress   (President)

ANSWER: President (House, Senate, and Congress are words about the legislative branch.)

1. say yes	confirm	approve	say no
2. senators	ambassadors	cabinet	judges
3. remove	leave	stay	resign
4. one-fourth	majority	51%	three-fourths

■ INFORMATION: Members of the Senate

There are 100 members in the Senate. Every state has two senators.

QUALIFICATIONS	REPRESENTS	SPECIAL DUTIES
Age: 30+ years U.S. Citizen: 9+ years Live: in state Term: 6 years Limit: none	Columbia • SOUTH CAROLINA entire state	• ratify/approve treaties • confirm appointments • try impeached officials

Using the Information

A. Work with a partner. Student A reads sentences 1–3. Student B answers True (**T**) or False (**F**).

STUDENT A	STUDENT B	
1. A senator's term is 4 years.	T	F
2. The Senate starts bills about taxes.	T	F
3. Senators must be at least 30 years old.	T	F

Switch roles. Student B reads sentences 4–6. Student A answers **T** or **F**.

STUDENT B	STUDENT A	
4. There are 100 senators.	T	F
5. Senators represent only one district.	T	F
6. The Senate ratifies treaties.	T	F

B. Three of the sentences above are false. Make them true. Rewrite them on the lines below.

_____.

_____.

_____.

READING: The Trial of Andrew Johnson

Only the House of Representatives can impeach officials. Only the Senate can **try** the officials. The Senate decides if the official can stay in office. The Senate does not try many impeached officials. In U.S. history, there was only one trial to **remove** a President from office. The President was Andrew Johnson. He was President (1865–1868) after the U.S. Civil War. The country had many problems. The President had many problems. Congress wanted to remove Andrew Johnson from the office of President.

Two-thirds (2/3) of the Senate must agree to remove an official from office. In 1865, there were 54 senators. Now there are 100 senators. At the trial against Andrew Johnson, only 35 senators voted to remove him. They needed 2/3 of 54 (or 36) votes. Andrew Johnson stayed in office.

Using the Reading

C. Now listen to your teacher tell you about the Senate votes in three cases. Remember there are 100 senators in Congress. Write the number of votes on the correct line. Answer the following questions. Circle **Y** (Yes) or **N** (No).

SENATE DUTY	NEED	CASE	VOTE	
			Yes	No
1. Try officials	2/3 majority	V.P. Kelly	____	____
2. Ratify treaties	2/3 majority	limit nuclear weapons	____	____
3. Confirm appointments	majority	Judge Bellos	____	____

1. Will the Senate remove the V.P. from office?   Y   N

2. Will the Senate ratify the treaty?   Y   N

3. Will the Senate confirm the judge?   Y   N

TESTING SKILLS

Circle the letter of the best answer:

1. There are _____ senators.
   a) 435   **b)** 100   **c)** 50

2. A senator's term is for _____ years.
   a) two   **b)** four   **c)** six

3. The Senate can ratify a _____ between the U.S. and foreign countries.
   a) law   **b)** tax   **c)** treaty

4. The _____ confirms appointments for judges.
   a) Senate   **b)** House   **c)** Cabinet

5. The Senate needs a _____ vote to remove an official from office.
   a) majority   **b)** 2/3   **c)** 3/4

REVIEW

Can you name . . .

- two qualifications of a senator?

- two special duties of the Senate?

- two senators from your state?

LESSON 15

Legislative Branch:
A Bill Becomes Law

OBJECTIVE | • Explain how a bill becomes a law

PRE-READING

Oral

Look at the picture below. Many families have rules for living together in their houses.

Work with a partner. Discuss these questions.

1. Do you have laws (or rules) in your home?
2. Who makes the rules in your home?
3. Do the rules change?

4. Do the laws of a country change?

5. Who makes the laws in the country your family came from?

Vocabulary

Read the sentences below.

A **committee** is a group of people. They work together.

You see a movie and you like it. You can **recommend** the movie to your friends.

Two candidates for President have different ideas. They can have a **debate.** They talk about their ideas.

Members of Congress are having a meeting today. They are in **session.**

The members will finish their meetings in December. They will **adjourn** the session and go home.

Members of Congress like a bill. They approve the bill. They **pass** it. Members of Congress do not like a bill. They do not approve the bill. They **defeat** it.

The President wants a bill to become law. He **signs** it. The President does not want a bill to be a law. He **vetoes** it.

The President vetoes a bill. Congress wants the law. Both the House and the Senate approve the bill with a 2/3 vote. They **override** the President's veto.

Written

The words on the left have the <u>opposite</u> meanings of the words on the right. They have very different meanings. Match the words on the left with the opposite on the right. Put the correct letter on the iine.

<u>C</u> **1.** in session

_____ **2.** pass

_____ **3.** sign

_____ **4.** debate

_____ **5.** recommend

_____ **6.** committee

a) defeat

b) say the same thing; agree

c) adjourned

d) say something is not good

e) one person works alone

f) veto

INFORMATION: A Bill Becomes Law

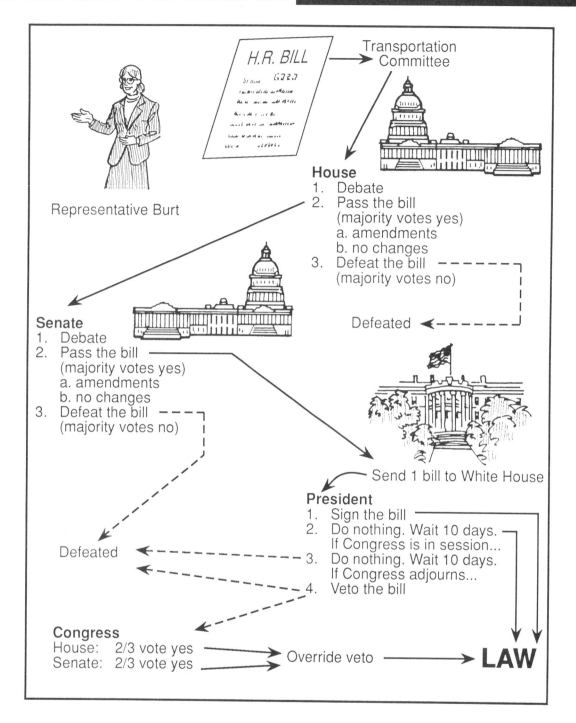

Using the Information

A. Form a small group. Read the sentences below. The sentences are <u>not</u> in the correct order. Discuss the correct order in your group. Put numbers 2–9 on the lines.

____ **a)** The House debates the bill.

____ **b)** The President signs the bill.

__1__ **c)** A representative starts a bill to repair highways.

_____ **d)** The bill goes to the Senate.

_____ **e)** The bill goes to the transportation committee.

_____ **f)** The House approves the bill with amendments.

_____ **g)** The Senate debates and approves the bill.

_____ **h)** The bill becomes law.

_____ **i)** The bill goes to the White House.

B. Form a small group. Pretend you are members of Congress. Would you approve the following bills? Why or why not? Share your group's answers with the class.

1. Change the speed limit from 55 MPH to 65 MPH on highways.
2. Give the army $10 million more.
3. Increase the number of immigrants coming to the U.S.
4. Lower all taxes.
5. Increase the price of stamps.

READING: The 1986 Immigration Law

It is usually a long process for a **bill** to become law. Sometimes a bill needs only one year to become law. But other bills need many years to become laws. For example, the 1986 immigration law took six years to become a law.

First, the House and the Senate started two different bills about immigration. There were many **debates** and changes to the two bills. After the debates, the House approved one bill and the Senate approved another bill. Next, they worked together to write one bill. The House and the Senate approved the bill. They sent the immigration bill to the President. Finally, the President **signed** the bill into law on November 6, 1986.

Using the Reading

C. Answer these questions:

1. Do bills usually become laws quickly?

2. Where did the immigration reform bill start?

3. What happened after the House and Senate approved the bill?

4. What was the President's final decision on the bill?

TESTING SKILLS

Read the first sentence. Circle the letter of the sentence with <u>the same meaning</u>.

1. The committee recommends the bill without changes.
   a) The committee amends the bill.
   b) The committee changes and recommends the bill.
   c) The committee recommends the bill. They do not change it.

2. It is usually a long process for a bill to become law.
   a) Sometimes it takes a long time for a bill to become law.
   b) Most of the time, it takes a long time for a bill to become law.
   c) It always takes a long time for a bill to become law.

3. Finally, the President signed the bill into law.
   a) In the end, the President signed the bill into law.
   b) Next, the President signed the bill into law.
   c) Before that, the President signed the bill into law.

REVIEW

Can you identify five steps necessary for a bill to become law? Use these words to help you:

bill starts   committee   debate   approve   sign or veto

LESSON 16

Judicial Branch: The Structure and the Appeals Process

OBJECTIVES | • Describe the organization of the judicial branch
| • Explain the appeals process

PRE-READING

Oral

Look at the following pictures. Take turns and describe the pictures. Do you think the people will go to a federal or state court?

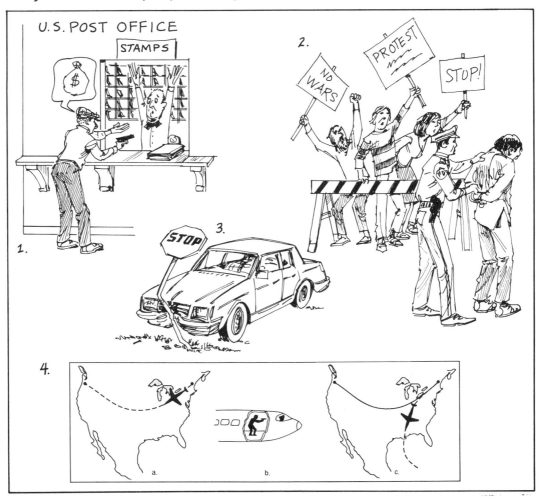

Vocabulary

Read the following vocabulary words:

(to) hear a case—a judge (and sometimes a jury) listens to both sides of a legal problem in court

decision—the result of a court case

(to) review—another judge (or group of judges) in a higher court looks at a decision; this judge (or these judges) decides if a decision is correct

(to) appeal—to ask another court to review a decision

appellate court—a court that hears appeals

District Courts—the lowest courts in the federal court system; they have a judge and jury; they hear the cases

Circuit Court of Appeals—appellate courts in the federal court system; they have a group of three judges to hear appeals; they do not have a jury

Supreme Court—the highest court in the U.S.; it has nine judges; all the decisions are final

(to) interpret—to decide if a law follows the Constitution

customs—taxes for imports (things people bring into the U.S. or things foreign companies want to sell in the U.S.)

Written

Scan this paragraph quickly and underline the following words:

interpret   appellate   review   case

Many federal courts are appellate courts. If someone does not like a decision from a lower court, that person can try to appeal. That person can ask an appellate court to review the case. If the case is about a federal law, the appellate court can interpret the law. So, the court decides if the law is constitutional.

number of times you see <u>interpret</u>   <u>1</u>

number of times you see <u>appellate</u>   ___

number of times you see <u>review</u>   ___

number of times you see <u>case</u>   + ___

                              Now add these numbers   = ___

Your answer = the number of articles in the Constitution.

INFORMATION: The Federal Court System

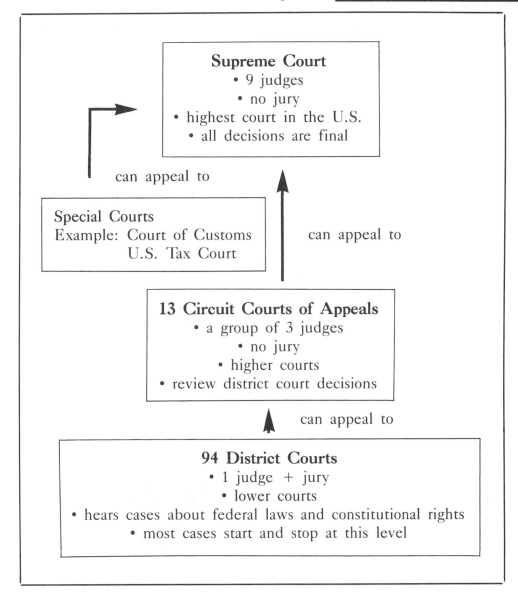

Using the Information

A. Listen to your teacher. Decide if the sentences are true or false. Circle **T** or **F**.

1.   T   F   (Look at picture #1 at the beginning of this lesson.)

2.   T   F   (Look at the diagram about the court system.)

3.   T   F   (Look at the diagram again.)

4.   T   F   (Look at picture #2 at the beginning of the lesson.)

5.   T   F   (Look at the diagram.)

B. Look at the diagram. Use appropriate words to complete the following:

There are ninety-four **1)** ___district___ courts in the federal

system. Congress can change this number. These courts

2) _____ cases about federal laws and

3) _____ rights. These are lower **4)** _____ .

Some cases go to higher courts. These courts are the

appellate courts. They hear **5)** _____ from district

courts. There are **6)** _____ Circuit Courts of Appeals

in the U.S.

Some very important cases can go to the **7)** _____

Court. It is the highest court in the U.S. There is only

8) _____ Supreme Court. The Constitution set up this

court.

Two examples of special courts are the Court of

9) _____ and the U.S. Tax Court.

READING: The Justice System

The following reading is from the *Federal Citizenship Text—U.S. Government Structure.* Try to read this paragraph.

"One of the most important rights in the U.S. is the right to a fair trial. The appeals process is set up to help make sure that people have as fair a trial as possible. Sometimes a person believes justice was not served at his / her trial because he / she believes:

- his / her rights were violated;
- a rule of law was not properly followed; or,
- all the evidence was not available.

That person may try to appeal his / her case to a higher court. The judge may agree with the:

- person and overturn the lower court's decision; or,
- lower court and uphold the decision.

The person may try to appeal again if he / she still is not satisfied. Courts will not always hear appeals, however."

Using the Reading

C. The paragraph above may be difficult to read. The following sentences are easier. They have the same information, but one is not correct. Can you find it? Put a check next to the wrong sentence.

1. We have the right to a fair trial.   _____

2. There is an appeals process to help us.   _____

3. If there is a problem at our trial, we can try to appeal.   _____

4. The problem can be about evidence (= information) in the case.   _____

5. The problem can be about our rights. Maybe the police did not follow rules.   _____

6. If we appeal, the appellate court always agrees with us.   _____

7. Sometimes the appellate court thinks the lower court was correct.   _____

8. The appellate court can say, "No, we will not review the case."   _____

TESTING SKILLS

Read (or listen to) this conversation. It is from an oral examination.

> JUDGE: Please explain the appellate review jurisdiction of the judicial branch.
>
> MS. MBUYI: I'm sorry. Could you please repeat?
>
> JUDGE: Okay. Please explain the appellate review jurisdiction of the judicial branch.
>
> MS. MBUYI: I don't understand "appellate review jur. . . ."
>
> JUDGE: The process of reviewing lower court decisions.
>
> MS. MBUYI: Oh, you mean like appeals?
>
> JUDGE: Yes, explain the appeals process.

Ms. Mbuyi asked for help understanding the questions in three ways. Try to find them.

Can you think of other ways to ask for help?

REVIEW

Pretend you are Ms. Mbuyi. Explain the appeals process.

The judge's next question will be: "What are the three types of federal courts?" Can you answer this?

LESSON 17

Judicial Branch: Duties of Federal Courts

OBJECTIVE | • Explain duties of federal courts

PRE-READING

Oral

Look at these pictures again:

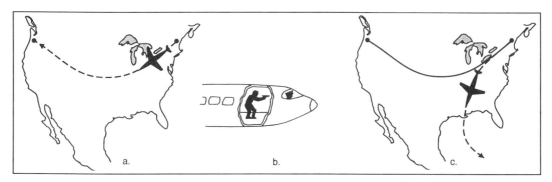

The man has a gun. He wants the pilot to fly to Cuba. He is hijacking the plane. Hijacking is a crime.

Discuss these questions:

Where did this happen?

Did it happen in a state?

Will they hear this case in a federal or state court?

Why?

Vocabulary

Complete the following crossword puzzle.

constitutional	**naturalization**	**ambassador**
lower	**laws**	**customs**

ACROSS

1 Federal district courts hear cases about _____ rights.
4 The process when an immigrant becomes a U.S. citizen.
5 An official representative of one government living in another country; the head of an embassy.

DOWN

1 People entering the U.S. have their suitcases searched by _____ officers, in airports, for example.
2 Rules of a government
3 The federal district courts are the _____ courts; the appeals courts are the higher courts.

INFORMATION: Duties of Federal Courts

These are the main duties of the federal courts:

- to hear cases about federal laws
- to hear cases about constitutional rights
- to guarantee the appeals process

These are the other duties of federal courts, which hear cases involving:

STATES	• between two states • between citizens of two states
FOREIGN GOVERNMENTS	• between a state government and a foreign government • between a U.S. citizen and a foreign citizen • if ambassadors have legal problems with the foreign government where he/she works
OTHER AREAS	• about problems with American ships • about special problems with federal taxes, customs, etc. • for naturalization

Using the Information

A. Unscramble these sentences. Use the chart on page 77. The first one is done as an example.

> EXAMPLE: cases / court / two / A / states / hears / between / federal
>
> A federal court hears cases between two states.

1. duty / courts / is / Naturalization / the / federal / of

_____

2. Cases / foreign tourists / federal / to / U.S. citizens / and / go / courts / between

_____

3. American / court / A / ships / hears / federal / cases / about

_____

B. Form a small group. Think of a problem for the federal courts. (For example, the hijacking situation goes to a federal court.) Discuss your problem with the class.

READING: The Federal Courts

Read the following paragraph. Then listen to your teacher read it. Five words are different. Underline the different words. Listen again. This time write the correct words.

We talked about twelve duties of the federal courts. They hear cases

about state laws. They interpret laws to see if they are constitutional.

They try to solve problems between tourists of two different states. If

a foreign office has a problem with the government of Florida, it can

bring a trial to a federal court.

TESTING SKILLS

Circle the letter of the best answer.

> **1.** What court can review a case?
> **a)** federal district court
> **b)** U.S. Customs Court
> **c)** appellate court

2. Which court has a jury?
   a) federal district court
   b) U.S. Circuit Court of Appeals
   c) Supreme Court

3. Which is <u>not</u> a case for a federal court?
   a) a case between two citizens of the same state
   b) a case between two citizens of different states
   c) a case between a foreign citizen and a U.S. citizen

REVIEW

Can you remember six duties of federal courts?

LESSON 18

Judicial Branch:
The Supreme Court

OBJECTIVE | • Explain the role of the Supreme Court

PRE-READING

Oral

Look at the picture of the Supreme Court below.

Discuss the court system in your country.

Does your country have a Supreme Court?

Does your country have an appeals process?

How does someone become a judge in your country?

Does your country have juries?

Vocabulary

Match the words on the left with the definition on the right. Put the correct letter on the line.

_____ 1. Justice

_____ 2. jury

_____ 3. judicial branch

_____ 4. Supreme Court

_____ 5. innocent

_____ 6. guilty

a) highest court in the U.S.
b) Decision: you did nothing wrong
c) court system of the U.S. government
d) a judge on the Supreme Court
e) Decision: you did something wrong
f) people who make a decision in a case

INFORMATION: The Supreme Court

The following picture shows the Supreme Court's bench. The Supreme Court is in Washington, D.C. The nine justices sit and listen to important cases.

- Nine justices
- Justices choose the cases to hear
- Supreme Court decisions are final
- Justices can say a state or federal law is unconstitutional

Using the Information

A. Read the following sentences. Are they true or false? Circle **T** or **F**.

1. You can appeal a Supreme Court decision.   T   F

2. The Supreme Court hears all appellate cases.   T   F

3. There is a jury and nine justices on the Supreme Court.   T   F

4. The Supreme Court listens only to cases about
federal laws.   T   F

5. The Supreme Court is in Washington, D.C.   T   F

READING: Supreme Court Justices

Supreme Court justices have an important job. Justices hear cases
about constitutional rights. Their decisions can affect all U.S. citizens.
One of the nine justices is the Chief Justice.

The President appoints someone to be a justice. The Senate must
approve the President's choice. Supreme Court justices have the
position until they die or retire. If justices do something wrong, the
Congress can try to impeach them. But, this does not happen very
often.

Using the Reading

B. Answer the following questions:

1. Who chooses a Supreme Court justice?

_____

2. What can happen if a justice does something wrong?

_____

3. How many Chief Justices are on the Supreme Court?

_____

4. If there is a new President, do all the Supreme Court
justices change?

_____

REVIEW

Do you know . . .

- how many justices are on the Supreme Court?
- two things the Supreme Court can do?

LESSON 19

Checks and Balances

OBJECTIVE | • Identify one way each branch of government checks and balances other branches

PRE-READING

Oral

Look at these pictures again. Can you identify these buildings?

Work with a partner. Discuss these questions:

1. What branch of the government does each building represent?

2. Can you identify one important duty of each branch?

3. Does one branch have more power than the others?

4. What is the federal government doing this month? Did you hear or read anything about taxes, court cases, defense, etc.?

Vocabulary

Read the following vocabulary words:

checks—restrictions on the duties of each branch

balances—separate powers to each branch

Complete the puzzle. Use the vocabulary from Lessons 1–18:

1. **C A B I N E T**
2. **H** _ _ _ _
3. **E** _ _ _ _ _ _ _ _
4. **C** _ _ _ _ _ _ _
5. **K** _ _ _
6. **S** _ _ _ _ _ _ _ _
7. **A** _ _ _ _ _ _ _ _ _
8. **N** _ _ _
9. **D** _ _ _ _ _ _ _
10. **B** _ _ _
11. **A** _ _ _ _ _ _ _ _ _
12. **L** _ _
13. **A** _ _ _ _ _ _
14. **N** _ _ _ _ _ _ _
15. **C** _ _ _ _ _ _ _
16. **E** _ _ _ _ _ _ _
17. **S** _ _ _ _ _ _

DEFINITIONS

1. The advisors to the President are called *cabinet* members.

2. There are 435 members in the _____.

3. The President and V.P. are part of the _____ branch.

4. The House and Senate together are called _____.

5. One title of nobility is _____.

6. The head of the Department of State is called _____ of State.

7. Changes to the Constitution are called _____.

8. The Army, _____, and Air Force are part of the military.

9. The lowest federal courts are _____ courts.

10. A plan or idea for a law is a _____.

11. The Senate must _____ treaties.

12. If Congress passes a bill and the President signs it, the bill becomes _____.

13. An _____ court reviews cases from lower courts.

14. Congress cannot give titles of _____.

15. During a _____ the candidates make many speeches.

16. Every 4 years there is an _____ for President and V.P.

17. The highest court in the U.S. is the _____ Court.

READING: Checks and Balances

The U.S. Constitution establishes three branches for the federal government: executive, legislative, and judicial. The three branches work together to help the country. Each branch has its own responsibilities and powers. No branch has more power than the other branches. They have balanced powers. Each branch has separate duties to check the powers of the other branches.

Using the Reading

A. Answer these questions:

1. Does one branch have more power than the other branches?

2. Do all three branches share many duties?

3. Will the President have more power than the courts in the future?

■ INFORMATION: Checks and Balances

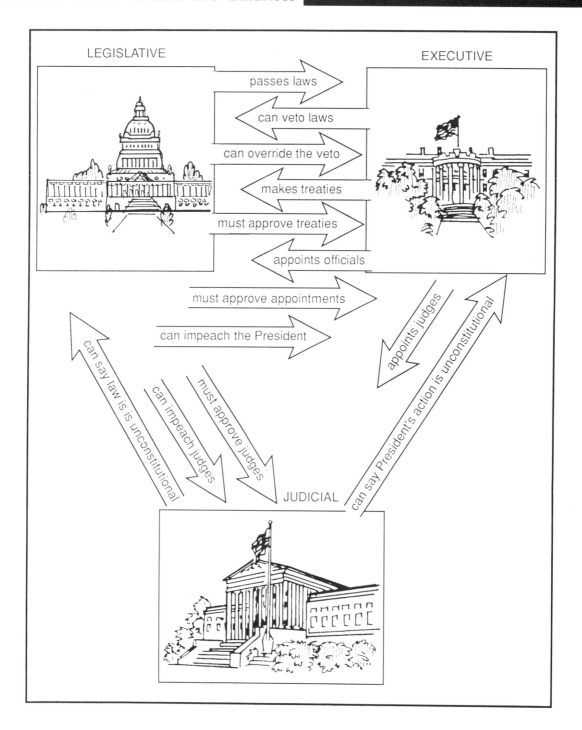

Using the Information

B. Look at the diagram and fill in the blanks in the sentences below.

    1. One of the important principles of the U.S. Constitution is

       the system of _____ and _____.

2. Congress can _____ laws, but the President can

_____ them.

3. The Supreme Court can say a law is _____.

4. The President _____ judges and the Senate must

_____ the appointments.

5. The legislative branch checks the executive and judicial

branches because it can _____ the President or a

judge from office.

C. Form a small group. Discuss these questions with the group:

1. Do you think checks and balances are important? Why or
why not?

2. Does the government of your country have checks and
balances?

3. What would happen in the U.S. if we did not have checks
and balances?

TESTING SKILLS

Read (or listen to) the following conversation.

INS OFFICIAL: What are the checks and balances?

MR. PEREZ: Checks and balances tell us about the powers of
the federal government . . . the three branches.

INS OFFICIAL: How do the three branches check and balance
each other?

MR. PEREZ: Let me think . . . the executive checks the
legislative.

INS OFFICIAL: How?

MR. PEREZ: Well . . . Congress can pass a bill, but the
President can . . . can . . . .

INS OFFICIAL: Can what?

MR. PEREZ: Say no . . . say no . . . I mean the President can
veto the bill.

Mr. Perez does not answer immediately. What words does he use to
get more time?

REVIEW

Can you explain . . .

- how the legislative checks the executive?
- how the executive checks the judicial?
- how the judicial checks the legislative?

LESSON 20

Review: The Federal Government

This lesson will help you review the information in Lessons 8–19. If you need help with these exercises, you can look back at the earlier lessons.

THREE BRANCHES OF THE FEDERAL GOVERNMENT

A. Complete the following crossword puzzle.

ACROSS

3 The federal government has _____ branches.
6 The executive branch enforces the _____.
9 No branch has more _____ than the other branches.
10 The head of the executive branch is the _____.
11 The Congress _____ the laws.

DOWN

1 Each branch has its own _____.
2 The branches have _____ powers.
4 One part of Congress is the _____ of Representatives.
5 The U.S. government has a system of _____ and balances.
7 The highest court in the U.S. is the _____ Court.
8 The second part of the Congress is the _____. (see 4, Down)

FEDERAL OFFICIALS

B. Work with a partner. One student will look at the chart on the top. The other student will look at the chart on the bottom. You can see that your chart is not complete. Do <u>not</u> look at your partner's chart. You can ask your partner questions to get the information you need. For example, you can ask, "How old does the Vice President have to be?" Complete the chart:

	PRESIDENT	V.P.	SENATOR	REPRESENTATIVE
Age	35+ years		30+ years	
Citizen		born in U.S.		7+ years
Residence		14+ years		in state
Term	4 years		6 years	
Limit	2 terms		none	
Number of:	1			435

	PRESIDENT	V.P.	SENATOR	REPRESENTATIVE
Age		35+ years		25+ years
Citizen	born in U.S.		9+ years	
Residence	14+ years		in state	
Term		4 years		2 years
Limit		none		none
Number of:		1	100	

CANDIDATES

C. Read the short descriptions of these candidates. Can they be candidates for President (Pres.), Vice President (V.P.), Senator (Sen.) or Representative (Rep.)? Look at the chart you completed on page 90. Put a check next to **all** of the offices they can be candidates for.

	PRES.	V.P.	SEN.	REP.
1. Amelia Soares, 40. Born in Brazil. U.S. citizen and living in Texas since 1960.	___	___	✓	✓
2. Rose Moradian, 60. Born in Hawaii. Living in Hawaii all her life.	___	___	___	___
3. James Carter, 60. Born in Georgia. Was U.S. President from 1977–1981.	___	___	___	___
4. Ronald Reagan, 74. Born in Illinois. Was U.S. President from 1981–1989.	___	___	___	___
5. Thomas Fondell, 29. Born in Minnesota. Living in Africa since 1980.	___	___	___	___
6. Elisabeth Bailey, 58. Born in Vermont. Living in Virginia since 1980.	___	___	___	___
7. Christine Purdy, 32. Born in Missouri. Living in Washington for 6 years.	___	___	___	___

Check your answers. Did the other students check the same offices?

FEDERAL CHECKS AND BALANCES

D. The three branches of government are represented by the buildings below. Fill in the name of each branch.

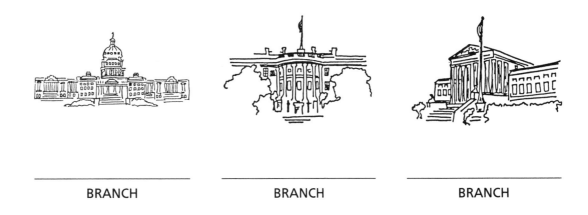

| BRANCH | BRANCH | BRANCH |

List three duties for each branch.

DUTIES:	DUTIES:	DUTIES:
1) _____	4) _____	7) _____
2) _____	5) _____	8) _____
3) _____	6) _____	9) _____

CHECKS AND BALANCES

Write one way each branch checks the other two branches.

CHECKS EXECUTIVE:	CHECKS LEGISLATIVE:	CHECKS LEGISLATIVE:
a) _____	c) _____	e) _____
CHECKS JUDICIAL:	CHECKS JUDICIAL:	CHECKS EXECUTIVE:
b) _____	d) _____	f) _____

OUR LEADERS TODAY

E. Find the names of some important leaders in the U.S. You can ask your family, friends, or teacher. You can hear about them on TV or read about them in the newspaper.

U.S. President _____

Vice President _____

Your Senators
    to Congress _____

_____

Your Representative
    to Congress _____

THE CABINET

F. The Cabinet members advise the President. Can you find in the puzzle on page 93 the names of the different Cabinet offices that are listed? Circle these words in the puzzle.

State

Labor

Health

Energy

Housing

Justice

Interior

Defense

Commerce

Treasury

Education

Agriculture

Transportation

```
H M Z T S D E F E N S E P R
E A I N T E R I O R W D O H
A G R I C U L T U R E U D O
L B B C F Z L E N T J C R U
T E S E I O A N R S U A N S
H W T Z X X B E A E S T I I
T R A N S P O R T A T I O N
S O T E E Z R G X W I O R G
T R E A S U R Y B U C N U O
C C A C O M M E R C E G H N
```

JUDICIAL BRANCH

G. The federal court system has 94 District Courts, 13 Circuit Courts of Appeals, and one Supreme Court.

Fill in the correct information:

First, a federal case starts in a _____ court.

Second, the case can be reviewed in an _____ court.

Third, if necessary, a final review can be made in the

_____ Court.

H. You are a Supreme Court Justice. Read the laws below. Are these laws constitutional? You must vote on each law. Write "Yes" if the law is constitutional. Write "No" if the law is unconstitutional.

VOTE

1. Today's President will become President for life. _____

2. All states will have the same number of senators. _____

3. The state of California can say "NO" to all new immigrants. _____

4. The people will vote for Supreme Court Justices.   _____

5. Every state will print money for that state.   _____

6. All citizens can have a lawyer.   _____

7. You must be a citizen for 10 years before you can vote.   _____

8. All children must pray in public schools.   _____

9. Newspapers can make jokes about the President.   _____

LESSON 21

State Government: Structure

OBJECTIVES
- Identify the structure of state governments
- Identify state leaders
- Explain direct democracy through referenda and petitions

PRE-READING

Oral

Look at the charts below. Discuss what is the same or different about them with a partner.

1787
U.S. Constitution Preamble . . . 3 branches Bill of Rights

1895
N.Y. Constitution Preamble . . . 3 branches Bill of Rights + more, such as: Right to join unions

Why do you think state constitutions are like the federal constitution?

Vocabulary

Read the following vocabulary words.

assembly—the name for the House of Representatives in some state legislatures

governor—the chief executive in a state

lieutenant governor—the assistant governor, the second-in-command in the state executive branch

National Guard—the military force of a state; the governor is the chief

petition—a voter (or group of voters) can write a paper (a petition) to explain a problem, ask for a new law, or change a law. A petition must have the signatures of many citizens before a state legislature will review it.

Written

Scan the Information below. Read quickly to answer these questions. Circle **Y** or **N**.

1. Do state governments have three branches of government?   Y   N

2. Does the head of a state have advisors?   Y   N

3. Are the Circuit Courts of Appeals part of the state court system?   Y   N

4. Do most states have two houses in the legislature?   Y   N

5. Can a state court hear cases about federal laws?   Y   N

INFORMATION: Three Branches of State Government

EXECUTIVE

Governor

• is chief of National Guard
• suggests state laws
• can veto state laws
• states have different terms, but usually
Governor = 2 or 4 years

Lieutenant Governor

• substitutes for the Governor if he or she is absent
or dies in office

Advisors: Attorney General, Secretary of State, Treasurer

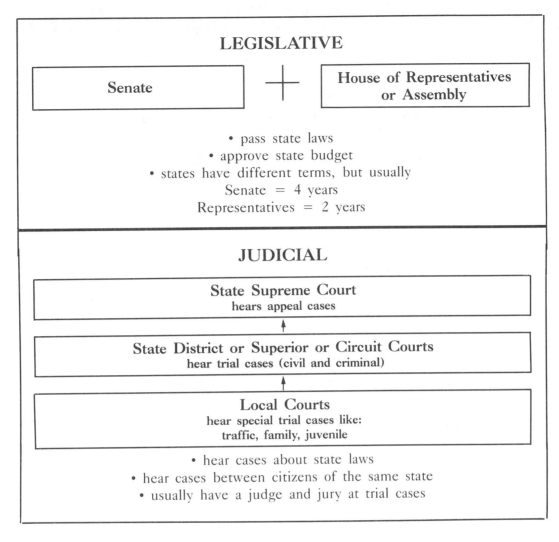

LEGISLATIVE

| Senate | ╪ | House of Representatives or Assembly |

- pass state laws
- approve state budget
- states have different terms, but usually
  Senate = 4 years
  Representatives = 2 years

JUDICIAL

State Supreme Court
hears appeal cases

↑

State District or Superior or Circuit Courts
hear trial cases (civil and criminal)

↑

Local Courts
hear special trial cases like:
traffic, family, juvenile

- hear cases about state laws
- hear cases between citizens of the same state
- usually have a judge and jury at trial cases

Using the Information

A. Work with a partner. This chart compares federal and state governments. Fill it in. Share your answers with the class.

FEDERAL GOVERNMENT	STATE GOVERNMENT
a) President	a)
b)	b) Chief of National Guard
c)	c) Lieutenant Governor
d)	d) State Supreme Court
e) Federal district courts	e)
f)	f) State Senate
g) House of Representatives	g)
h) Separation of powers	h)

▉ READING: Direct Democracy

Sometimes the federal government seems far away. Many citizens think they cannot change the federal laws. They think their Senators and Representatives do not pay much attention to their ideas. For the state government, the situation is different. This government is closer. State officials listen to opinions of the citizens.

One example of direct democracy is the right to petition. The citizens take action themselves. A petition to the state government can ask to make a new law or to change a present law. The idea from the petition is put on a ballot. Every voter can vote on it. If citizens agree with the idea, they vote "yes." If they disagree, they vote "no."

Using the Reading

B. Are the following sentences true or false? Circle **T** or **F**. Correct all the false sentences.

1. A petition is an example of direct democracy.　　　　T　　F
2. Many citizens think they can change federal laws easily.　　　　T　　F
3. Sometimes, citizens of a state vote to make changes in state laws.　　　　T　　F
4. Petitions can ask only for new laws.　　　　T　　F

TESTING SKILLS

Listen to (or read) the following conversation. Circle the letter of the best response for Raul.

QUESTIONER: Okay, let's talk about state governments. Why does your state use a state constitution and the federal Constitution?

RAUL: **1. a)** Because the federal one is for all the states, but the state one has more things just about my state.

b) I don't know.

c) We only have to use the state constitution.

QUESTIONER: What is the name for the leader of a state?

RAUL: **2. a)** I think we call him the President.

b) The Lieutenant Governor helps him.

c) It is Governor.

QUESTIONER: How are state governments set up?

RAUL: **3. a)** They are like the federal government. They have a constitution and three branches.

b) They have a president, senators, and representatives.

c) State governments set up taxes.

QUESTIONER: Do states have a system of checks and balances?

RAUL: **4. a)** I'm not sure, but I think so because they all have three branches.

b) I'm not sure. Our teacher didn't tell us about it.

c) I'm not sure. Do they?

QUESTIONER: How are state governments different from the federal government?

RAUL: **5. a)** State governments are exactly the same as the federal government.

b) State governments are more like a direct democracy.

c) The federal government makes state laws.

REVIEW

Who is your Governor? Write the name here: _____

Do you know your State Senator or Representative / Assemblyman?

Write the name(s) here: _____

_____

Can you explain an example of direct democracy?

Can you name one duty for each branch of the state government?

What do you call the highest STATE court?

LESSON 22

State Government: Responsibilities

OBJECTIVES
- Identify services provided by the states
- Compare state and federal responsibilities

PRE-READING

Oral

Look at the pictures below. Does a state government or a federal government have responsibility? Talk with your partner and decide.

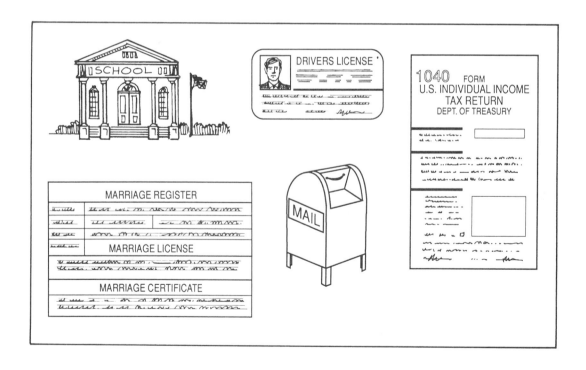

Discuss your opinions with the class.

Do the state and federal governments share any responsibilities? What are they?

Written

Read the sentences below. Which ones do you think are true about state governments? Put a check next to the true sentences.

_____ **1.** State governments have responsibility for state transportation.

_____ **2.** The head of a state is the President.

_____ **3.** The Constitution says the states have powers.

_____ **4.** Police departments are part of the state responsibility.

_____ **5.** The Post Office is a state responsibility.

Vocabulary

One word does not belong with the others. Circle it.

1. responsibility   duty   power   petition

2. international   local   federal   state

3. post office   army   police   treaties

4. Arizona   Texas   Oregon   Los Angeles

READING: State Government Responsibilities

Amendment 10 of the U.S. Constitution says: If the federal government does not have certain powers in the Constitution, then the states or the people do. For example, the states have responsibilities for establishing education systems and police departments. They build roads and control licenses for marriage, driving, and some jobs (like doctors and lawyers). They make rules about trade inside the states.

Sometimes the state and federal governments share responsibilities. Many times they both offer services to help people, like health care and welfare. They also protect our environment, like parks and rivers. Federal and state governments can collect taxes, establish courts, and make laws. There is one important point to remember: No state law can go against the U.S. Constitution!

Using the Reading

A. Use the information in the paragraphs to fill in the chart below. List four responsibilities for each side.

STATE RESPONSIBILITIES ALONE	SHARED FEDERAL & STATE RESPONSIBILITIES
1) _____	1) _____
2) _____	2) _____
3) _____	3) _____
4) _____	4) _____

B. Here is a list of state licenses:

driver   child care worker   lawyer
marriage   doctor   selling alcohol

Form several groups in class. Choose one of the licenses and discuss some rules for it. Think about age, training, testing, and why the license is important.

Share your ideas with the class. Discuss the other groups' ideas. Do you agree with them? Would you add something else?

TESTING SKILLS

Read the following questions. Discuss them with a partner. You can write the answers if you want.

1. How many states are in the U.S.?

   _____

2. What is one responsibility for the state government, but not for the federal government?

   _____

3. Does the Constitution give powers to the states?

   _____

4. Why do both state and federal governments collect taxes?

   _____

REVIEW

Look back at the first two exercises on page 101. Were your choices correct?

Can you explain the correct answers?

LESSON 23

Local Government: Structures

OBJECTIVES
- Identify types of local governments
- Name local leaders

PRE-READING

Oral

Look at the following pictures.

Work with a partner. Discuss these questions.

1. Do you live in a city, town, or rural area?
2. In your country, did you live in a city, town, or rural area?

3. Who were the local leaders?

4. Who are your local leaders now?

5. Where can you find out their names?

Vocabulary

Write a simple definition for these words. Use your dictionary.

EXAMPLE: **board** *a committee with a special responsibility*

1. mayor _____

2. council (city council) _____

_____

3. manager (city manager) _____

_____

4. county _____

5. commission (county or city commission) _____

_____

6. commissioner _____

7. supervisor (county supervisor) _____

_____

8. charter (local government charter) _____

_____

INFORMATION: Types of Local Government

Local governments are different from state and federal governments because they do <u>not</u> have constitutions. Local governments receive a charter (plan of government) from the state government. There are different types of local governments: city, county, town, and village. The local **charter** tells about the organization for the government. Look at this chart. What kind of local government do you have?

CITY

1. MAYOR–CITY COUNCIL
• The mayor and council are elected by the citizens.
• The mayor is the executive. The council is the legislature.

2. COUNCIL–CITY MANAGER
• The council is elected. The council hires a city manager.
• The council makes the laws and directs the city manager. The city manager carries out the city's business.

3. COMMISSION
• The citizens elect a group of commissioners.
• The commission is both an executive and a legislature.

COUNTY

COUNTY BOARD OR
BOARD OF COMMISSIONERS OR BOARD OF SUPERVISORS
• Citizens elect members to the board.
• County governments usually do not have 3 branches. The board makes plans for the county and enforces state laws.

Using the Information

A. Look at this list of government officials. One is not elected. Put a check next to that official:

_____ **1.** city mayor   _____ **4.** city commissioner

_____ **2.** city council   _____ **5.** county board member

_____ **3.** city manager   _____ **6.** county supervisor

B. Form a small group. Look at the boxes. These people want to be the mayor of a small city in the U.S. Talk about the qualifications of these people. Then, choose the person you think will be the best mayor. Be prepared to tell the class your reasons.

ESTHER APPOLO, 30	GORDON BELTZ, 59
• administrator	• computer programmer
• 4 years on city council	• 5 years on city council
• wants to stop crime in city	• wants to lower city taxes

MARIO GALLO, 52
- doctor
- 12 years on Board of Health
- wants to build new hospitals and clinics

JUDITH ROBERTS, 65
- retired teacher
- 25 years with schools
- wants to pay city employees more wages

ISAAC WILLIAMS, 68
- retired policeman
- 20 years as Police Chief
- wants to stop crime

EDNA SIMASO, 50
- lawyer
- 10 years on School Board
- wants to lower taxes

Group choice for mayor _____

Reason _____

Class choice for mayor _____

READING: The Court System

Read this paragraph from the *Federal Citizenship Text—U.S. Government Structure:*

"Local governments have a court system, which handles local issues, such as traffic laws and small claims. Sometimes cases may be **appealed** to the state courts. Judges in local courts are sometimes called justices of the peace, though many are called judge or magistrate. Local courts tend to specialize in one area of law, such as traffic or family, to make sure that the judge is as knowledgeable as possible. By specializing, local courts try to provide responsive, efficient legal service."

Using the Reading

C. Now read the sentences below. They have the same information, but they are easier to understand. Discuss the answers to the questions about your local government.

1. Local courts take care of local problems. For example, you go to a traffic court for traffic problems. If the money in the case is a small amount, you go to a small claims court.
   - What kinds of local courts are in your area?

2. Sometimes a citizen can appeal a local court decision to a higher state court. For example, the county court says you

are guilty in an accident. You do not believe you are guilty. You want a review. You can appeal to a higher court in your state.

• Can you think of another situation?

3. Judges in local courts are called justices of the peace, magistrates, or judges.

• What are they called in your local courts?

TESTING SKILLS

This conversation is part of an INS interview. Think about the answers to the questions. Practice the interview with your partner.

INS OFFICIAL: Where do you live?

APPLICANT: _____

INS OFFICIAL: What kind of local government do you have?

APPLICANT: _____

INS OFFICIAL: Who are your local leaders?

APPLICANT: _____

INS OFFICIAL: Have you ever been to a local court?

APPLICANT: _____

REVIEW

Who are your local leaders?

LESSON 24

Local Government: Responsibilities

OBJECTIVE | • Identify services provided by local governments

PRE-READING

Oral

These six pictures represent services from local governments. Discuss the pictures with a partner. Write a word or sentence to describe the service. Share your answers with the class.

Vocabulary

Use your dictionary to help you understand the words below. Match the words on the left with the definitions on the right. Put the correct letter on the line.

_____ **1. funding**

_____ **2. license**

_____ **3. (to) hire**

_____ **4. (to) collect**

_____ **5. traffic**

_____ **6. records**

_____ **7. (to) rescue**

_____ **8. local**

_____ **9. safe**

_____ **10. curriculum**

a) what we teach in schools

b) not dangerous

c) moving cars, buses, etc.

d) to save from danger

e) to give someone a job

f) official papers or documents

g) near where you live

h) to pick up together

i) money for a program

j) permission to do something, like driving

INFORMATION: Local Services

Situation	Name	Responsibilities
1.	Water Department	makes sure drinking water is safe
2.	Roads/Highway Department	repairs local roads, signs, and bridges
3.	Board of Education	hires teachers, decides salaries, curriculum, funding
4.	Clerk's Office	keeps records (marriage licenses, birth certificates)
5.	Sanitation Department	collects trash, keeps area clean
6.	Fire & Rescue Department	stops fires, saves people in emergencies
7.	Police Department	protects people, makes sure laws are not broken
8.	Treasury or Tax Department	collects money to provide for services and programs
9.	Courthouse	hears cases about local laws, family problems, traffic laws
10.		

Using the Information

A. Read about some local problems. Look at the chart on page 110. Decide where to call for help. Write the name of the local service.

1. Steve sees some smoke coming from his neighbor's apartment.

   Where can he call? _____

2. Ali lives on a very busy street. There are lots of accidents on the corner. Ali thinks the town needs a stop sign on the corner.

   Where can he call? _____

3. Mary wants to go to Brazil. She needs a passport. She needs some identification to show she is a U.S. citizen.

   Where can she call? _____

4. Ana sees a very drunk man. He is leaving a bar. He is going to drive his car.

   Where can she call? _____

5. Pheng's son does not understand English. He is having problems in school. He needs help to learn English.

   Where can he call? _____

6.

B. Form a small group. Can you think of another service provided by your local government? Add it to box 10 on the chart. Can you think of another problem? Add it to number 6 above. Share your group's ideas with the other groups in the class.

READING: Public Schools

Read the following paragraph from the *Federal Citizenship Text—U. S. Government Structure:*

"One of the most important functions or duties of local government is managing the public schools. People often want to be involved in decisions made about the schools because they want the children in the area to get a good education. Local school districts elect school boards so that the people can be involved. The school board makes decisions about teacher salaries, curriculum, and, to a certain extent, funding, as well as many other administrative aspects of maintaining the schools in its district. People in the community often go to school board meetings to publicly state their opinions about what needs to be done in the schools."

Using the Reading

C. Form a small group. Pretend you are a group of parents. You are going to a school board meeting. Make a list of five more things you want the school to do. Your list can include new ideas, too. Be prepared to tell the school board your reasons.

	NEED	REASON
1.	Bilingual Aides	Some students do not speak enough English.
2.	_____	
3.	_____	
4.	_____	
5.	_____	
6.	_____	

TESTING SKILLS

Read the first sentence in each question below. Circle the letter of the sentence below it that has <u>the same meaning</u>.

1. Local governments offer many services.
   a) Local governments take care of schools, roads, and water.
   b) Local governments pay the state for services.
   c) Local governments receive services from the federal government.

2. The people elect members to the local school board.
   a) The people hire the school board members.
   b) School boards have elected members.
   c) School boards have appointed members.

3. The County Courthouse hears cases about traffic laws.
   a) Local courts hear cases about buying school buses.
   b) Local courts hear cases about the price of stamps.
   c) Local courts hear cases about speeding tickets.

4. The Clerk's Office keeps official records.
    a) The Clerk's Office takes care of licenses and certificates.
    b) The Clerk's Office gives driving tests.
    c) The Clerk's Office keeps tax money.

REVIEW

Name three services your local government provides.

LESSON 25

General Review

This lesson will help you review the information in Lessons 1–24.

LEADERS

A. We have different names for many leaders in our three levels of government. There is a list of those names below. Can you find the names in the word search? Circle the words.

President

Governor

Representative

Senator

Assemblyman

Mayor

City Council

Supervisor

Justice

Officials

```
M  A  Y  S  S  R  Z  J  U  S  T  I  C  E  E
O  F  N  E  U  B  R  E  P  R  E  S  I  U  V
F  V  Z  N  P  R  E  S  I  D  E  N  T  U  S
F  G  O  A  E  V  U  B  J  Z  M  A  Y  O  R
I  E  N  T  R  M  H  J  X  Y  P  R  C  D  N
C  A  G  O  V  E  R  N  O  R  R  I  O  U  N
I  X  G  R  I  M  A  X  I  C  E  A  U  L  X
A  N  A  S  S  E  M  B  L  Y  M  A  N  I  S
L  A  X  D  O  K  C  C  E  A  Y  X  C  Z  P
S  R  E  P  R  E  S  E  N  T  A  T  I  V  E
P  E  S  A  R  D  B  O  U  C  I  L  L  E  V
```

PETITIONS

B. Form a small group. Choose one topic:

1. You want to change a law in your state.
2. You want to write a new law.
3. You want the state or local government to give money to build a hospital or school or more roads.

114

Discuss your choice. If you want one of these things to happen, what can you do? Write a group petition. Say what you want. Give your reasons. Give ideas to make this happen.

Share your petition with the class. Do your classmates agree with your ideas? Have a class vote on each petition.

RESPONSIBILITIES OF GOVERNMENT

C. Look at the following list. These are responsibilities or actions of the different levels of government. List them in the correct column in the chart below.

passes state laws

School Board of Education

National Guard

driver's licenses

makes treaties

parking ticket

prints money

city council

gives money for defense

collects federal taxes

water department

cases between citizens of two states

cases between citizens of same state

rules for trade in one state

rules for international trade

fire department

Federal	State	Local

THE CONSTITUTION

D. Complete the crossword puzzle below.

ACROSS

2 The Bill of Rights includes the first _____ amendments.

5 The U.S. Constitution is the _____, or supreme, law of the land.

7 Freedom of _____ means we can say our thoughts.

8 If we bring a case to court, we can have a _____ help us.

DOWN

1 The U.S. government has separation of _____.

2 The U.S. has _____ branches of government.

3 The Constitution lists the basic _____ for all people living in the U.S.

4 The Constitution says we have a government by the _____.

6 At a trial, a group of citizens, or _____, can listen to our case.

IMPORTANT DOCUMENTS

E. Read the following phrases. They can be found in different official documents. Match the phrase on the left with its document on the right. Put the correct letter on the line.

_____ **1.** "We the people of the United States . . ."

_____ **2.** "The citizens will elect a governor every 4 years . . ."

a) Articles of the Constitution

b) Bill of Rights

c) Amendments 11–26

d) Preamble

_____ **3.** "The mayor and city council will be the executive and legislative branches . . ."

_____ **4.** ". . . freedom of religion, speech, press . . ."

_____ **5.** ". . . citizens 18 years or older can vote . . ."

_____ **6.** "As of February 3, 1991, first class letters need a 29¢ stamp."

_____ **7.** "Everyone must pass a driving test to get a license."

_____ **8.** "Three-fourths (3/4) of the states must vote to amend the Constitution."

e) a state constitution

f) a state law

g) a local charter

h) a federal law

NUMBER GAME

F. You need to remember some important numbers in the U.S. Government. Fill in the blanks below with the correct numbers:

1. branches in the U.S. Government _____3_____
2. senators in the U.S. Congress _____
3. representatives in the U.S. Congress _____
4. Vice President(s) in the executive branch _____
5. Supreme Court Justices _____
6. states _____
7. amendments in the Bill of Rights _____
8. George Washington was President # _____. _____
9. In 1987, the U.S. Constitution was _____ years old + _____

Now add these numbers = _____

Your answer has three numbers. Each number represents a letter. Use the chart below. Find the numbers from your answer and their letters.

0	1	2	3	4	5	6	7	8	9
S	E	P	D	O	T	L	R	U	A

Write the letters in the same order. You will see the name of a special place for you.

___ ___ ___

Study Questions

After you finish this book, you should try to answer these questions. Be prepared to answer these questions when you go to the INS for a citizenship examination.

THE CONSTITUTION

1. When was the Constitution written?
2. Why is the Constitution called the "supreme law of the land"?
3. Who does the Constitution guarantee basic rights for?
4. Name one of the main principles of the Constitution.
5. How can we change the Constitution?
6. What are the first ten amendments called?
7. Name one right guaranteed by the first amendment.
8. What is your right if you are accused of a crime?
9. Who has the right to vote?

FEDERAL

1. What are the three branches of government?
2. Which branch of the government has the offices of the President and Vice President?
3. Name one duty of the President.
4. Name one qualification to be President.
5. How often do we have elections for President?
6. A person can be President for how many terms?
7. Why do we have a Vice President?
8. Name one qualification to be Vice President.
9. Name one duty for a Vice President.
10. What is the Cabinet?

11. What does the Cabinet do?

12. Name one Cabinet department.

13. Which branch of the federal government makes the laws?

14. What do we call the two houses of Congress?

15. Tell one duty of the House of Representatives.

16. Tell one duty of the Senate.

17. Name one thing the Constitution says the Congress <u>cannot</u> do.

18. How many Senators are in Congress?

19. Name one qualification to be a Senator.

20. How many Representatives are in Congress?

21. Name one qualification to be a Representative.

22. Where does the Congress meet?

23. Which branch of government interprets the laws?

24. Name the highest court in the U.S.

25. What special power does the Supreme Court have?

26. Name one duty of federal courts.

27. What can you do if you do not think you had a fair trial?

28. What is one way each branch of government checks and balances other branches?

29. Who is the U.S. President now?

30. Who is the U.S. Vice President now?

31. Who is your Representative to Congress?

32. Name one of your Senators to Congress.

STATE

1. Name one service offered by state governments.

2. What is an example of direct democracy in state governments?

3. How many branches are in the state government?

4. What do we call the head of the executive branch in a state government?

5. Name one duty of a governor.

6. Name one duty of the state legislature.

7. Name one duty of a state court.

8. Who is the governor of your State?

LOCAL

1. Name two services offered by local governments.

2. Who is the head of your local government?

Vocabulary Index

PART TWO

CITIZENSHIP
EDUCATION

LESSON 1

Responsibilities and Rights
of Citizens

OBJECTIVE | • Identify specific duties and rights of citizens

PRE-READING

Oral

Look at the pictures below. They show some of the responsibilities of U.S. citizens.

Discuss the following questions with the class.

1. What are five responsibilities you see in the pictures?

2. Which responsibilities are the same in your country?

3. What other responsibilities do you have in your country?

4. Are there other responsibilities for U.S. citizens?

Vocabulary

Match the words on the left with the definitions on the right. Put the correct letter on the line. You can use a dictionary for help.

_____ **1. duty**

_____ **2.** (to) **register**

_____ **3.** (to) **obey**

_____ **4. protection**

a) to follow laws or rules

b) safety; taking care of someone or something

c) something you have to do; responsibility

d) to put your name on a list

READING: Rights of U.S. Citizens

The U.S. Constitution and the Bill of Rights protect the rights of all people living in the U.S. There are some other rights for U.S. citizens only. Amendments 11–26 of the U.S. Constitution tell us some of the extra rights for citizens (see *U.S. Government Structure,* Lesson 6).

Who is a U.S. citizen? A person born in the U.S. is a citizen. If a U.S. citizen has a baby in another country, the baby may be a U.S. citizen. Resident aliens can become citizens after they live legally in the U.S. for 3 to 5 years and take a citizenship exam. If they pass the exam, they can become naturalized citizens (see Lesson 5 for more information).

Both U.S.-born and naturalized citizens have many extra rights. Only citizens can vote in U.S. elections. They can work for the federal government. They can travel with U.S. passports. They can apply to bring their family to the U.S. Only citizens can be members of a jury.

Naturalized citizens do not have <u>one</u> special right. Naturalized citizens cannot become President or Vice President of the U.S. But, a naturalized citizen can be a senator, representative, governor, mayor, etc.

Using the Reading

A. Unscramble the following sentences. Look at the Reading to help you. The first word of each sentence has a capital letter. The first sentence is done for you.

1. citizens / some / are / for / There / only / rights /

There are some rights only for citizens.

2. is / in / born / a / A / U.S. / the / person / citizen /

_____.

3. vote / citizens / Only / can / elections / in /

_____.

4. U.S. / travel / with / They / passport / can / a /

_____.

5. President / U.S. / citizens / Naturalized / cannot / of / Vice
President / become / the / or /

_____

_____.

■ INFORMATION: Duties of U.S. Citizens and Why They Are Important ■

Duties	Why?
Obey laws	Laws protect the people. A basic right for all people is protection.
Vote	The U.S. is a representative democracy. All citizens have to vote to choose good people to be representatives.
Pay taxes	The government needs money to pay for services (for example, police and military protection).
Be on a jury when called	Everyone has the right to a trial with a jury (6th Amendment). Members of a jury must be U.S. citizens.
Register with the military[1]	If there is a war, the military will need soldiers.

[1]This is a duty for men only. All men must register when they become 18 years old.

Using the Information

B. The Information chart tells you about the duties of U.S. citizens. It also tells you the reason these duties are important. You will use some charts in other lessons. It is important to learn the best way to read a chart.

1. At the top of every chart, you will find a title. What is the title of this chart? _____.

2. This chart has two columns. You read <u>down</u> a column. Each column has a heading. The heading tells you about the information in the column. The first column is about

   Duties. How many duties do you see? _____

3. What is the heading of the second column? _____

4. Now, look at the whole chart. Read <u>across</u> the lines. Why do citizens have to vote? _____

5. Why do citizens have to be part of a jury? _____

   _____

6. Sometimes you will see a little number next to a word. Find the word "military" in the column **Duties.** This number is a *footnote*. A footnote tells you there is more information. Sometimes the footnotes are on the bottom of a page. Sometimes the footnotes are in the back of a book or lesson. Where is the footnote for this Information

   chart? _____

7. What do you learn from footnote 1? _____

   _____

C. Form a small group. Discuss the following questions with your group. Then share your group's answers with the class.

1. When do people pay taxes in the U.S.?
2. What kind of taxes do people pay in the U.S.?
3. What does the government do with our tax money?
4. Do you think U.S. taxes are higher or lower than taxes in other countries?

TESTING SKILLS

Sometimes the INS official will ask you questions you do not understand. Sometimes you will have problems remembering the answer immediately. What should you do?

Read (or listen to) the following conversation:

INS OFFICIAL: Does everyone have the same rights in the U.S.?

KYUNG: Everyone . . . ?

INS OFFICIAL: Yes, everyone, all the people living in the U.S. Do all the people have the same rights?

KYUNG: Oh, I understand now. No, citizens have some special rights.

INS OFFICIAL: Can you tell me one of those rights?

KYUNG: Let me think . . . I think one special right is . . . is . . . only citizens can vote.

INS OFFICIAL: Okay. And what are some duties of citizens?

Think about these questions:

1. Did Kyung answer the first question immediately?
2. Why did he repeat "Everyone"?
3. Why did he say "Let me think . . ."?
4. If you do not know an answer immediately, what do you say? Do you ever say, "Let me think . . ."?
5. Answer the last question for Kyung.

REVIEW

Name three special rights for citizens.

Name five duties for citizens.

LESSON 2

Voting

OBJECTIVES
- Identify who has the right to vote
- Explain the importance of voting in a democracy

PRE-READING

Oral

Work with a partner. Look at the picture below.

Read about the people in the picture. Decide if each person can vote. Share your decisions with the class.

- Mr. Curtis, 37, was born in Michigan. He is learning to read and write at the Union Adult Center. Can he vote?

- Mr. Marino, 45, was born in Wisconsin. He lost his leg in the Vietnam War. He cannot walk. Can he vote?

- Mr. Lee, 89, is from Hong Kong. He became a U.S. citizen in 1987. Can he vote?

- Nicole Reville, 28, is from Haiti. She is studying U.S. History. She wants to take the citizenship examination next month. Can she vote?
- Manuel Otero, 18, was born in Florida. He will finish high school in May. Can he vote?
- Ms. Repetto, 52, is from Arizona. She wants to be the mayor of Union City. Can she vote?

Vocabulary

Read the definitions and sentences below.

candidate—a person who wants to be elected
In 1988, George Bush and Michael Dukakis were **candidates** for President of the U.S.

convicted—found guilty of a crime
Mr. Smith was **convicted** of killing a policeman.

(to) deny—to refuse to give something; to say "no"; not allow
INS can **deny** you citizenship if you lie on the application.

issue—an important point that people vote on or discuss
Child care is an important **issue** for many families in the U.S.

privilege—a special right only for some people; a special favor
In some countries, rich people have more **privileges** than others.

rational—able to reason; sane
Rational people think carefully before they make decisions.

(to) require—to demand; to make something necessary; to need
Every state **requires** people to have a driver's license before they drive a car.

Use some of the new words to complete the following sentences.

1. The government _____ people to pay taxes.

2. There is usually more than one _____ in a national election in the U.S.

3. An employer cannot _____ you a job because of your religion.

4. You will have to go to jail or pay a fine if you are

   _____ of a crime.

READING 1: Voting Laws

The U.S. Constitution protects many voting rights, but it does not **require** people to vote. State governments make the laws about voting in their own states. The states can require people to live in the state for a certain period of time before they vote in state and local elections. But the states cannot require citizens to pass a reading and writing test.

The Constitution says states <u>cannot</u> **deny** the right to vote to citizens:

- who are 18+ years old
- because of race, color, or sex
- because they did not pay a voting tax
- in national elections for President and Vice President

States <u>can</u> **deny** the right to vote to citizens:

- who have been **convicted** of serious crimes
- who cannot make **rational** decisions

Using the Reading

A. Work with a partner. Student A reads sentences 1–3. Student B listens and says if they are true (**T**) or false (**F**).

    EXAMPLE: State governments make some voting laws.   T   F

STUDENT A	STUDENT B
1. The U.S. Constitution gives the right to vote to citizens of all races and sexes.	T F
2. Citizens must pass a reading and writing test before they can vote.	T F
3. States can require citizens to pay a voting tax.	T F

Switch roles. Student B reads sentences 4–6. Student A listens and says if they are **T** or **F**.

STUDENT B	STUDENT A
4. The U.S. Constitution gives the right to vote to citizens of all ages.	T F
5. People who are convicted of serious crimes can lose the right to vote.	T F
6. If a citizen moved to Kansas in August 1988, he/she could not vote for President in November 1988.	T F

B. Four of the sentences above are false. Rewrite the four sentences on the lines below. Make them true sentences.

_____

_____

_____

_____

READING 2: Voting—A Duty and a Privilege

One of the most important rights for U.S. citizens is the right to vote. Voting is a duty in a representative democracy. All citizens should vote to choose good people to be the federal, state, and local leaders. Voting is also a **privilege** because not everyone can vote.

Before citizens vote, they must register to vote in their state. You can register in places like local libraries and courthouses. You do not have to pay to register.

Everyone should also learn about the **candidates** and **issues** in the election. We can get information by reading newspapers or listening to the news on TV and the radio. We can go to political meetings. Freedom of speech, the press, and assembly (1st Amendment) help us learn about the candidates and issues.

We have a *government of the people*. The people must be active. They must work with organizations to make their communities and states better. Voters must make good decisions. The people we elect will have a lot of control. They will decide:

- what laws to pass,
- how much tax we will pay, and
- what services we will receive.

Using the Reading

C. Use the following words to write questions. You will have to add some words. The first one is done for you.

1. What / one / important / right / U.S. citizens ?
   What is one important right for U.S. citizens?

2. Why / voting / important / U.S. ?

   _____

3. What / citizens / do / before / they / vote ?

   _____

4. How / citizens / information / candidates / issues ?

_____

5. Why / important / elect / good / leaders ?

_____

Work with a partner. Ask your partner to answer the questions.

TESTING SKILLS

Circle the letter of the best answer to complete the following sentences.

1. A citizen's right to vote is _____ by the U.S. Constitution.
   a) denied
   b) protected
   c) required
   d) taxed

2. States can require citizens to _____ before they vote.
   a) pass a reading and writing test
   b) pay a voting tax
   c) register
   d) be over 19 years old

3. Voting is _____ in the U.S.
   a) controlled only by the federal government
   b) a right for all people living
   c) required by law
   d) a duty and a privilege

4. The people we elect will decide _____.
   a) who will be the next President
   b) what laws to pass
   c) if we can go to political meetings
   d) if we can read newspapers

REVIEW

Explain . . .

- who can vote in the U.S.
- what you must do before you can vote.
- why voting is important in the U.S.

LESSON 3

Requirements for Naturalization

OBJECTIVE | • Identify the requirements to apply for naturalization

PRE-READING

Oral

Form a small group. Read the list below. These are some reasons people want to become U.S. citizens.

Can you think of two other reasons? Write them below.

1. They want to vote.
2. They want to bring some other members of their family to the U.S.
3. They want to help their communities.

4.

5.

Some people cannot become U.S. citizens. Here are two reasons. Can you think of three more reasons? Write them below and at the top of page 138.

1. The person has lived in the U.S. for only two years.
2. The person broke some laws in the U.S. and went to jail for one year.

3.

4.

5.

Vocabulary

Read the definitions of the following words and terms.

Communist Party—a political group or party; the group believes people should not own private property and the government should control the production and distribution of things the people need.

(to) **deport**—to make someone who is not a citizen leave a country

dictator—the head of a country; this person has all the power and makes all the laws

(to) **gamble**—to take chances with money; to make or lose money by playing cards, games, horses, etc.

oath of allegiance—a serious promise to be loyal

good moral character—the qualities of a person who behaves in a lawful and correct way, according to the rules of society

Written

Read the following situations about permanent residents. Do you think the person can apply for citizenship? Check (√) **Yes** or **No**.

	YES	NO
1. Juanita came to the U.S. 2 years ago.	____	____
2. Sam is a good worker and is studying English and about the U.S. government.	____	____
3. Omar thinks the U.S. form of government is not good. He is a member of the Communist Party.	____	____
4. Makiesse is 17 years old. She came to the U.S. 6 years ago.	____	____

INFORMATION: The Requirements for Naturalization

There are many requirements to become a U.S. citizen. These are the most important ones:

> You must:
> * Be 18+ years old
> * Be a Permanent Resident for 5 years or more[2]
> * Be loyal to the U.S.
> * Be able to read, write, speak, and understand basic English
> * Have good moral character
> * Understand the U.S. government structure and the Constitution
> * Take an oath of allegiance to the U.S.

Using the Information

A. Complete the following exercise. Look at the chart to find the words to write in the blanks.

If you want to apply for **1)** _____, you must be 18 **2)** _____ old or more. You must be a permanent **3)** _____ for 5 years or more. This means you have lived legally in the U.S. for at least **4)** _____ years.

You must know some **5)** _____ so you can read speak, and write it. You must also know about the U.S. **6)** _____ and about the U.S. Constitution. It is important to be loyal to your new country and to take an **7)** _____ of allegiance. Another requirement is to have good moral **8)** _____. This means you are not a bad person.

████ **READING: Requirements to Apply for Naturalization** ████

Immigrants must meet certain requirements when they apply for naturalization. For example, they must be at least 18 years old and be legal residents of the U.S. for at least 5 years. They apply for naturalization in the state where they live. They must live in that state for the *last 6 months* (or more) of those 5 years. They do not have to live in the U.S. every day for 5 years, but they cannot live outside the U.S. for:

---

[2]See the Reading about special cases.

a) a period of 1 year or more, or

b) a total of 30 months or more.

Many immigrants ask about the requirement for **good moral character.** The INS explains that to become a U.S. citizen a person cannot be someone who:

a) drinks too much;

b) is married to two or more people at the same time;

c) sells his or her body for sexual pleasure;

d) buys, sells, or uses drugs;

e) **gambles** illegally;

f) is a criminal;

g) was convicted of a crime in the U.S. and was in jail for 6+ months;

h) was convicted of killing another person without a legal reason;

i) was a member of a **Communist Party** during the 10 years before applying for naturalization (except if forced to join, or under 16 years old);

j) wants a **dictator** to rule the U.S., or wants to use violence against the U.S. government or government officers; or,

k) the government is trying to **deport.**

The INS also thinks about the age of the people applying for naturalization. If someone is 50 years old and has lived in the U.S. for 20+ years as a permanent resident, that person does not have to meet the English language requirement.

There are some special cases for applying. Some of the requirements are different for husbands, wives, and children of U.S. citizens. For example, husbands and wives have to live in the U.S. for only 3 years before applying for citizenship. Also, if someone worked for the U.S. military or for organizations helping the U.S. in other countries, the requirements for that person are different.

Using the Reading

B. Read the situations about permanent residents again. Use the Information and the Reading. Can the person apply for citizenship? Check (√) **Yes** or **No**.

	YES	NO
1. Juanita came to the U.S. 2 years ago.	____	____
2. Sam is a good worker and is studying English and about the U.S. government. He has worked in Michigan for 7 years.	____	____

3. Omar thinks the U.S. form of government is not good. He is a member of the Communist Party.   ____ ____

4. Makiesse is 17 years old. She came to the U.S. 6 years ago.   ____ ____

Here are some more situations:

5. Henri is married to Caroline. Caroline is a U.S. citizen. Henri has lived in the U.S. for 4 years.   ____ ____

6. Jan does not work. Jan steals things from stores and sells them. Jan went to jail for 10 months last year.   ____ ____

7. Ferdosi came to the U.S. when she was 14. Now she is 20. She goes to college and works part-time at a hospital. Her friends say she is a good person.   ____ ____

8. Estella became a permanent resident 7 years ago. She lived in California for many years. Three months ago she moved to Virginia. She works as a computer programmer. She does not gamble or use drugs.   ____ ____

9. Karol is from Bulgaria. He became a permanent resident 5 years ago. He works with his brother as a house painter. Karol never learned English. He speaks only Bulgarian with his brother. Karol is loyal to the U.S. He does not like the Communists.   ____ ____

C. Work with a partner. Think about five friends who are immigrants living in the U.S.

Does each friend meet all these requirements? Write their names in the box below. Put a check (√) under the requirements they meet.

NAME	AGE	PERMANENT RESIDENT	YEARS OF RESIDENCE	GOOD CHARACTER	KNOWS ENGLISH	KNOWS GOVT[3]
1.						
2.						
3.						
4.						
5.						

[3]Govt = Government

TESTING SKILLS

Bernadette is applying for citizenship. Read (or listen to) the following conversation between Bernadette and an INS official. Circle the letter of the best response for Bernadette.

INS OFFICIAL: Let me ask you some questions about the requirements for citizenship. When did you obtain legal status as a resident alien in the U.S.?

BERNADETTE: **1. a)** I think it is next year.

b) I'm not sure I understand. Do you mean as a permanent resident?

c) I don't know. Did I become a citizen?

INS OFFICIAL: Yes. When did you become a permanent resident?

BERNADETTE: **2. a)** Eight years ago.

b) I will be a permanent resident when I am a citizen.

c) I came to the U.S. with my sister and brother.

INS OFFICIAL: That's good. You meet the permanent resident requirement. Now, are you over 18 years old?

BERNADETTE: **3. a)** I don't remember.

b) Yes, I am.

c) I live in Florida.

INS OFFICIAL: Okay, do you use drugs or gamble?

BERNADETTE: **4. a)** Would you please repeat the question?

b) Gambling is taking chances with money.

c) Drugs are not good.

INS OFFICIAL: Do you use drugs, like cocaine, or gamble illegally to make money?

BERNADETTE: **5. a)** It is important to make money in America.

b) I don't know, maybe.

c) No, I don't.

INS OFFICIAL: How long have you lived at your present address?

BERNADETTE: **6. a)** I live at 672 N. 1st Avenue.

b) For 2 years.

c) I came to America when I was 22.

REVIEW

Name five important requirements for naturalization.

LESSON 4

The Application Process

OBJECTIVES
- Explain the application process for naturalization
- Describe an interview between an applicant and an INS official

PRE-READING

Oral

Look at the picture below.

A person is filling out a form to apply for naturalization.

Work with a partner. What questions do you think are on the form? Write four or more. Share them with the class.

1) _____

2) _____

3) _____

4) _____

Vocabulary

The INS identifies some important papers by letters and numbers. Read the following explanations.

144

N-400—the four-page INS application form for naturalization

G-325—the two-page biographic (or personal) information form; also necessary for the application; the INS sends this form to the FBI

N-405—the INS form filed at court after passing the interview and examination

Use these words to complete the crossword puzzle below. You can use a dictionary to help you.

applicant   **certificate**   **fingerprint**   **interview**
   biographic   **dictation**   **hearing**

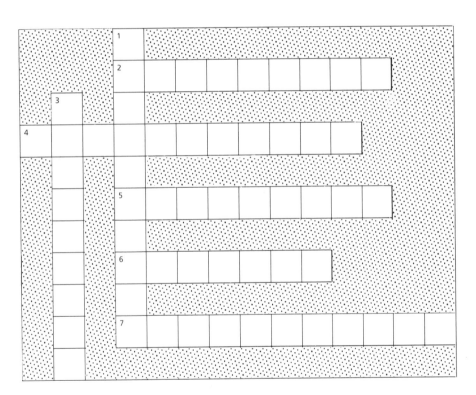

ACROSS

2 a meeting; someone asks you questions to find out information
4 the mark or pattern on the inside of the tip of your finger; the police look at this to identify people
5 a person who applies for something
6 an official meeting in court with a judge
7 an official paper; someone receives this when he or she completes something like a school course

DOWN

1 personal; about a person's life
3 a common exercise for students; a teacher reads a sentence or paragraph aloud and students write it

INFORMATION: The Application Process to Become a Citizen

1.

Fill out application forms (N-400, G-325)

2.

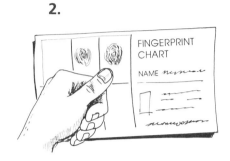

Have police or INS put fingerprints on chart

3.

Turn in or mail forms, fingerprint chart, and three photos to INS office

4.

Get a letter in the mail to go to INS office

5.

Have interview/ examination with an INS official

6.

Pay $50.00 to file the N-405 form at court

7.

Get a letter in the mail to go to court for a citizenship hearing

8.

Final Hearing—take the oath of allegiance

9.

New U.S. Citizen—get the certificate of naturalization

Using the Information

A. Read the following sentences. They are not in the correct order. Look at the diagram of the application process. Write the number for the sentences in the correct order. The first one is done for you.

_8_ **a)** At court, the applicant says the oath of allegiance.

____ **b)** The applicant pays a fee of $50.00 for the N-405 form.

____ **c)** The applicant completes two INS forms: N-400 and G-325.

____ **d)** The applicant has an interview and naturalization examination with an INS official.

____ **e)** The applicant goes to a police station (or INS office) and puts his or her fingerprints on the application chart.

____ **f)** The applicant receives a letter. It tells the applicant to go to court at a specific date and time.

____ **g)** The applicant brings or mails all the forms and three photos to the local INS office.

____ **h)** The applicant gets a certificate of naturalization. It says the applicant is a U.S. citizen.

____ **i)** The INS sends a letter to the applicant. It tells the applicant the time and day for the interview.

B. There are four words in the Information diagram with the same meaning as the four words below. Write the words on the lines.

1. complete _____   **3.** receive _____

2. bring to _____   **4.** say (the oath) _____

READING: An Interview and Naturalization Examination

If the **applicant** completes the forms correctly, an INS official asks the applicant to come for an **interview**. The interview is very important. Part of the interview can be an oral examination.

First, the applicant takes an oath to tell the truth. Then the official checks the **biographic** information on the application forms. The official asks the applicant some of the same questions. The official wants to be sure the applicant did not lie or misunderstand the questions.

Second, the official must decide if the applicant understands English. If the applicant can answer the official's questions, the official knows the applicant can *understand* and *speak* English. The official also checks if the applicant can *write* English. The official can give the applicant a **dictation**. Usually the dictation is only one sentence to write.

Third, the official checks the applicant's knowledge of the U.S. government. The official can ask questions about the government, the Constitution, and about U.S. history. Sometimes the applicant takes a written examination about these subjects.

If the applicant passes the English and government examinations and answers all the questions correctly, the official completes the **N-405** form. The applicant pays a $50.00 court fee and waits for a letter about the court **hearing**.

If the INS official does not think the applicant is ready, the official will tell the court the applicant should not become a citizen at that time. The applicant can:

1. be rescheduled for another examination at a later date; or,
2. go to the court and ask the judge to make the decision about citizenship.

Using the Reading

C. Work with a partner. Role-play an interview. One person is an INS official and the other person is an applicant. Ask the applicant five questions about his or her life and five questions about U.S. government and history. Dictate a simple sentence for the applicant to write.

Switch roles. The first applicant becomes the official. Ask five questions about his or her life and five questions about U.S. government and history. Dictate a sentence.

TESTING SKILLS

Circle the letter of the best answer.

1. Where do applicants turn in the application for naturalization forms?
   a) at court
   b) at the INS office
   c) at the police station
2. When does an applicant have an interview with an INS official?
   a) before the applicant fills out the forms
   b) when the applicant puts his or her fingerprints on the chart

c) after the applicant turns in the forms and receives a letter

3. If the applicant has a good interview and passes the naturalization examination, what happens?

    a) The applicant pays $50.00 to file the N-405 application.

    b) The applicant shakes hands with the official and becomes a citizen.

    c) The applicant brings three photos to the INS office.

4. What does the INS official check during the interview?

    a) the information on the application form only

    b) the information on the application form and the applicant's knowledge of English only

    c) the information on the application form and the applicant's knowledge of English, U.S. government, and U.S. history

REVIEW

Explain the application process to become a citizen. Use these words to help you:

    application forms   **fingerprints**   **turn in**

    interview / examination   **pay $50.00**   **hearing**   **certificate**

LESSON 5

The Court Hearing

OBJECTIVES
- Explain the oath of allegiance
- Explain the final court hearing

PRE-READING

Oral

Look at the picture below. It shows people taking the oath of allegiance. Discuss the following questions with a partner.

1. Where are the people?
2. Are the people all about the same age?

3. Do you think the people come from the same country?

4. Who is giving them the oath?

5. Why do they raise their right hands?

6. What happens after they finish saying the oath?

READING 1: The Oath of Allegiance

The oath of allegiance is very old. The U.S. government started using it in the 1790's. Many words are not used frequently today. (You will see the oath in Reading 2.) The following sentences explain the oath.

- I give up my past citizenship and my loyalty to my other country and its leader(s).
- I will support and defend the U.S. Constitution and all U.S. laws against enemies at home and in other countries.
- I will be loyal to the U.S.
- I will fight for the U.S. if the law tells me to fight.
- I will help the military with non-fighting work if the law tells me to help.
- I will do important national work outside of the military if the law tells me to.
- I accept these duties. No one is forcing me to become a citizen. I do not have any doubts about becoming a citizen.
- Because I am telling the truth, I will sign my name.

Using the Reading

A. Read the sentences below about the oath of allegiance and becoming a citizen. Circle **T** (true) or **F** (false).

1. You can become a U.S. citizen and continue being a citizen of another country. T F

2. As a citizen you will fight in the army when necessary by law. T F

3. As a citizen you do not have to follow the U.S. Constitution. T F

4. You will help protect the U.S. from enemies. T F

5. You have to work for the military, if the law tells you. T F

6. As a citizen you can be loyal to the ruler of another country. T F

Vocabulary

Match the words on the left with the definitions on the right. Put the correct letter on the line. You can use a dictionary to help you. The first one is done for you.

<u>C</u> **1.** (to) **affix**

_____ **2.** (to) **declare**

_____ **3.** (to) **perform**

_____ **4.** (to) **renounce**

_____ **5.** (to) **bear arms**

_____ **6. noncombatant**

_____ **7. potentate**

_____ **8. sovereignty**

_____ **9. evasion**

_____ **10. mental reservation**

a) independent country
b) to give up
c) to put in place
d) action or plan <u>not</u> to do something
e) to say
f) leader of a country
g) to carry guns, to fight
h) doubts, uncertainty
i) not fighting
j) to do

READING 2: The Oath of Allegiance

Scan the following paragraph. Find the words below in the paragraph. Circle them.

declare   defend   arms   service   obligation

OATH OF ALLEGIANCE

"I hereby declare, on oath, that I absolutely and entirely renounce and abjure all allegiance and fidelity to any foreign prince, potentate, state, or sovereignty of whom or which I have heretofore been a subject or citizen; that I will support and defend the Constitution and the laws of the United States of America against all enemies, foreign and domestic; that I will bear true faith and allegiance to the same; that I will bear arms on behalf of the United States when required by law; that I will perform noncombatant service in the Armed Forces when required by law; that I will perform work of national importance under civilian direction when required by law; and that I take this obligation freely without any mental reservation or purpose of evasion: SO HELP ME GOD. In acknowledgment whereof I have hereunto affixed my signature."

Using the Reading

B. Listen to your teacher read the oath aloud. Many of the words are difficult to pronounce. Practice reading it aloud with a partner.

INFORMATION: The Final Court Hearing

Some applicants do not pass the naturalization examination the first time. Some applicants need to improve their English. Some need to learn more about the U.S. government. Applicants may take the exam several times, if necessary.

When the applicants pass the examination, they wait for a letter from the INS about the final hearing at court. This letter tells them the time, date, and place of the hearing.

What to bring:
 — the official letter about the hearing
 — other INS documents listed in the letter, for example:
   • the alien registration card, and
   • INS travel papers

Where to go:
 Each local INS office decides the place.
 — Most hearings are at federal courthouses.
 — Some hearings with many people are in large rooms (auditoriums) in public buildings.

What to do:
 — Take the oath of allegiance.
 — Sign the INS document.
 — Return alien registration cards, INS travel documents, etc.
 — Receive a certificate of naturalization.

Using the Information

C. Work with a partner. Partner A looks at this page. Partner B looks at the next page.

Partner A reads the first paragraph aloud to Partner B two or three times. First, Partner B listens. Then, as Partner A reads again, Partner B writes the missing words on the blanks.

Switch roles. Partner B reads the second paragraph aloud to Partner A two or three times. First, Partner A listens. Then, Partner A writes the missing words on the blanks.

Partner A

Read aloud:

After you pass the naturalization examination, you will receive a letter. This letter tells you to come to court at a specific time and date. You must bring several papers with you. Some of the papers are your alien registration card and your INS travel documents. You should bring the letter too.

Listen, then write:

You will probably go to your **6)** _____ at a federal

courthouse. Some other people will be there too. All of you will

become **7)** _____ together. You raise your right hand and

take the **8)** _____ of allegiance. Then you turn in the INS

papers. Finally you will receive your **9)** _____ of

naturalization. Congratulations! You are now a **10)** _____

U.S. citizen.

Partner B

Listen, then write:

After you pass the naturalization **1)** _____, you will receive a letter. This letter tells you to come to **2)** _____ at a specific time and date. You must **3)** _____ several papers with you. Some of the papers are your **4)** _____ registration card and your INS **5)** _____ documents. You should bring the letter too.

Read aloud:

You will probably go to your hearing at a federal courthouse. Some other people will be there too. All of you will become citizens together. You raise your right hand and take the oath of allegiance. Then you turn in the INS papers. Finally you will receive your certificate of naturalization. Congratulations! You are now a new U.S. citizen.

D. Contact your local INS office and ask these questions.

1. Where do you have the hearings for citizenship?
2. How many times each year do you have hearings?
3. About how many people become citizens at one time?
4. How many people became citizens last year from your INS office?

Report the answers to the class. See if your classmates received the same information.

TESTING SKILLS

Read the following sentences. Circle the letter of the sentence below it that has <u>the same meaning</u>.

1. Applicants may take the exam several times, if necessary.

   a) Applicants must pass the exam the first time.

   b) Applicants take several different exams.

   c) Applicants can take the exam more than one time.

2. At the hearing you take an oath of allegiance.

   a) At the hearing you take an examination.

   b) At the hearing you promise to be loyal to the U.S.

   c) At the hearing you read the Bill of Rights aloud.

3. You will receive a certificate of naturalization.

    a) An INS official will give you a paper saying you are a U.S. citizen.

    b) An INS official will give you travel documents.

    c) An INS official will give you an alien registration card.

4. I will fight for the U.S. if the law tells me to fight.

    a) I will become a U.S. soldier if necessary by law.

    b) I will fight another U.S. citizen if necessary.

    c) I must work in the military before I become a citizen.

REVIEW

Name two things you bring to the hearing:

1. L __ t __ __ r

2. A __ i __ n __ e __ __ s __ __ at __ __ __ C __ r __

Name two things you do at the hearing:

1. Take an _____ of _____

2. Receive a _____ of _____

LESSON 6

National Symbols

OBJECTIVE | • Identify ten national symbols

PRE-READING

Oral

Look at the pictures below. Write the names from the list under the pictures you know.

White House　　**U.S. Capitol**　　**Liberty Bell**　　**Lincoln Memorial**

Vocabulary

Read the definitions of the following words.

exhibit—a collection of objects usually found in a museum; the objects can be letters, things from a house, clothing, musical instruments, photographs, paintings, etc.

People look at exhibits in museums to find out information about a subject like the Civil War or the history of immigration in the U.S.

inauguration—the ceremony when the President takes office

The 20th amendment says each inauguration for President must be on January 20th.

memorial—a building or statue to remember a famous person or time in history

The Vietnam Memorial in Washington, D.C., is a long black wall with a list of names of people who died during the Vietnam War.

monument—like a memorial; a building to remember someone or something important

Many tourists like to visit the national monuments in the U.S.

pledge—a promise; like an oath

Many children say the Pledge of Allegiance to the U.S. flag in school.

statue—an object made to look like or represent a person; usually made of stone, wood, or metal

One park in Washington, D.C., has a statue of George Washington sitting on a horse.

symbol—something that represents something else

The flag is often a symbol for a country. "$" is a symbol for U.S. money.

INFORMATION 1: Four National Symbols of the U.S.

THE AMERICAN FLAG

- 13 stripes: 7 red and 6 white for the first 13 states.
- 50 stars (one for each state).
- Represents freedom and justice.

THE STATUE OF LIBERTY

- Symbol for immigrants—many immigrants saw this statue when they arrived by boat.
- Represents freedom, opportunity, and international friendship.
- In New York City.

INDEPENDENCE HALL

• Meeting place for the Continental Congresses[4] before the War for Independence and for the first government of the U.S.

• Declaration of Independence and U.S. Constitution written and signed here.

• In Philadelphia.

LIBERTY BELL

• Symbol of freedom.

• Rang on July 4, 1776, for our national holiday, Independence Day.

• Has a famous crack.

• In Independence Hall (Philadelphia).

Using the Information

A. Write the answers to the following questions.

   1. Which national symbol is found near New York City?

   2. What do the stripes on the U.S. flag represent?

   3. Where was the Declaration of Independence signed?

4See the U.S. History textbook, Lessons 5, 7, and 8.

READING 1: The American Flag and the Statue of Liberty

Many people around the world know the American Flag. It has three names: *Old Glory, Stars and Stripes*, and the *Star-Spangled Banner*. The third name is also the name of our national song.[5]

The flag represents freedom and justice in the U.S. It has three colors: red, white, and blue. There are 13 red and white stripes. These stripes represent the original 13 states in the United States of America. There is a field of blue with white stars. In 1990 there were 50 stars. Each star represents one of the states in the U.S.

People put up flags on special holidays. Government office buildings put up a flag every morning and take it down every evening. There are special ways to take care of the U.S. flag.

Students say the Pledge of Allegiance to the flag in many schools. This is the pledge: *I pledge allegiance to the flag of the United States of America and to the Republic for which it stands, one nation, under God, indivisible, with liberty and justice for all.* This pledge says you are loyal to the U.S. and the states are united as one nation with liberty and justice for everyone.

The Statue of Liberty was a gift from France in 1886. It represents freedom, opportunity for Americans, and international friendship. In the early 1900's, many immigrants came by boat to the U.S. They saw the statue on an island near New York City. It was their first sight of America.

There is a museum in the bottom part of the statue. It has exhibits about the history of immigration in the U.S. There are many pictures, letters, and objects from the native countries of the immigrants.

Using the Reading

B. Bring a picture or drawing of your country's flag to class. Tell the class about your flag. These are some questions to think about:

> What do the colors of the flag represent?
>
> If there is a picture on the flag, what does it represent?
>
> Are there special times when people put up flags in your country?

C. Listen to your teacher read the Pledge of Allegiance aloud. Practice reading it aloud with a partner.

---

[5]See the U.S. History textbook, Lesson 13.

INFORMATION 2: Six National Symbols in Washington, D.C.

THE U.S. CAPITOL

- Meeting place for the U.S. Congress: Senate and House of Representatives.
- Place for the inauguration of most Presidents.

THE WHITE HOUSE

- Official home for Presidents (except George Washington).
- Address: 1600 Pennsylvania Ave.
- Burned during War of 1812 and rebuilt after the war.

WASHINGTON MONUMENT

- Built to remember George Washington, the first President.
- 555 feet high.
- Visitors may go up inside the building.

LINCOLN MEMORIAL

- Built to remember Abraham Lincoln, the 16th President.
- Has a very large statue of Lincoln sitting in it.
- Has two famous speeches by Lincoln on the walls.

JEFFERSON MEMORIAL

- Built to remember Thomas Jefferson, the third President.
- Has a large statue of Jefferson standing.

NATIONAL ARCHIVES

- Has exhibits with the original Declaration of Independence, the U.S. Constitution, and the Bill of Rights.
- It protects and keeps other important documents.

Using the Information

D. Read the sentences below. Circle **T** (true) or **F** (false).

1. The President lives at the U.S. Capitol.   T   F
2. The U.S. Capitol is in Washington, D.C.   T   F
3. The Declaration of Independence was signed at the National Archives.   T   F
4. The Washington Monument is a statue of George Washington.   T   F
5. Some memorials in Washington, D.C., honor U.S. Presidents.   T   F
6. You can find some of Abraham Lincoln's speeches on the walls of his memorial.   T   F

READING 2: The U.S. Capitol and the White House

Two important buildings in Washington, D.C., are national **symbols.** The U.S. Capitol is a symbol for our legislative branch of government. The Senators and the Representatives meet at the Capitol. They make the laws for the U.S. Every four years, on January 20th, we have an

inauguration ceremony for the President. Most inaugurations are in the Capitol.

The White House is the symbol for the executive branch of our government. It is the home and office for the President. The President often meets his advisors, members of Congress, and representatives from foreign governments at the White House. Special dinners and events take place at the White House.

Using the Reading

E. Work with a small group. Complete the following chart. Think about three different countries.

COUNTRY	HOME FOR THE LEADER	PLACE FOR MAKING LAWS	NAME OF ONE NATIONAL SYMBOL

TESTING SKILLS

Role play an interview with an INS officer. Work with a partner.

Ask your partner to tell you a few sentences about two of the national symbols. Switch roles. Your partner asks you about two other symbols.

REVIEW

Name three national symbols that represent a person.

The J __ __ F __ __ S __ __ MEMORIAL

The L __ __ __ O __ N MEMORIAL

The __ __ S H __ __ __ T __ N MONUMENT

Name three national symbols that have or had government offices.

The W __ __ T __ H __ U __ __

The U __ C __ __ I __ O __

I __ D __ __ E __ D __ N __ __ H __ __ L

Write down one of the names for the American flag.

LESSON 7

Review

A. Vocabulary. Complete the following puzzle. Use words from Lessons 1–6. The definitions are below. The first letter of each word is given to you.

1. D _ _ _

2. E _ _ _ _ _ _ _ _ _

3. M _ _ _ _ _ _ _

4. O _ _ _

5. C _ _ _ _ _ _ _ _ _ _ _

6. R _ _ _ _ _

7. A _ _ _ _ _ _ _ _ _

8. C _ _ _ _ _ _ _ _ _

9. Y _ _ _ _

1. A responsibility; something you have to do

2. A test

3. Army, Navy, Air Force, and Marine Corps

4. A serious promise

5. A plan of government—it tells about the form of government, laws, and rights

6. Basic things people <u>can</u> do

7. Loyalty; support to government, country, or leader

8. An official paper; you receive this when you become a citizen

9. Citizens must be 18 _____ or older to vote in the U.S.

B. U.S. Government. Work with a partner. Partner A looks at the paragraphs below: *U.S. Constitution A.* Partner B looks at the paragraphs on the next page: *U.S. Constitution B.*

Partner A reads the first paragraph aloud to Partner B two or three times. First, Partner B listens. Then, as Partner A reads again, Partner B writes the missing words on the blanks.

Switch roles. Partner B reads the second paragraph aloud to Partner A two or three times. First, Partner A listens. Then, Partner A writes the missing words on the blanks.

U.S. Constitution A

The U.S. Constitution says the U.S. is a democracy. The people help make the decisions. The citizens choose leaders or representatives to work in the government. The federal government has three branches with different duties. No person or part of the government has too much power (see *U.S. Government Structure,* Lesson 19).

The Constitution is the supreme **7)** _____ of the country. It tells the important rules of the U.S. It **8)** _____ the rights of **9)** _____ people living in the U.S. The Bill of **10)** _____ lists many of our most important rights. The U.S. Constitution is a **11)** _____ Constitution because the people and representatives can make **12)** _____ and additions to the Constitution.

U.S. Constitution B

The U.S. Constitution says the U.S. is a **1)** _____. The people help **2)** _____ the decisions. The **3)** _____ choose leaders or representatives to work in the government. The federal government has **4)** _____ branches with different **5)** _____. No person or part of the government has too much **6)** _____ (see *U.S. Government Structure,* Lesson 19).

The Constitution is the supreme law of the country. It tells the important rules of the U.S. It protects the rights of all people living in the U.S. The Bill of Rights lists many of our most important rights. The U.S. Constitution is a living Constitution because the people and representatives can make changes and additions to the Constitution.

C. Voting Issues. Make a list of important issues today. For example, in 1990 some of the local and national issues were:

1. Should the government pay for child care?
2. Should abortion be legal or illegal?
3. Should the local government spend more money on roads and highways?
4. Should the government make taxes higher to pay for more services?

Write three or four other important issues below.

1) _____

2) _____

3) _____

4) _____

Discuss:

As a class, choose one issue for discussion and voting.

First, form a small group. Work together like a political party (a political party is a group of people with similar ideas about government—politics, economics, social issues, etc.). Discuss your ideas about the issue above. Make a group decision about the issue. (You can use the space below to write your group's ideas.)

Second, plan an election. Choose one person to be the candidate for your group. Have a class discussion about the issue. Your candidate tells your group's decision. Listen to all the candidates. Vote for the candidate with the best ideas about the issue.

D. Applying for Citizenship. Work with a partner. Look at these pictures about applying for citizenship. They are not in the correct order. Discuss each picture. Put the pictures in the correct order. Write the numbers 1–9 on the lines under the pictures. The first one is done for you.

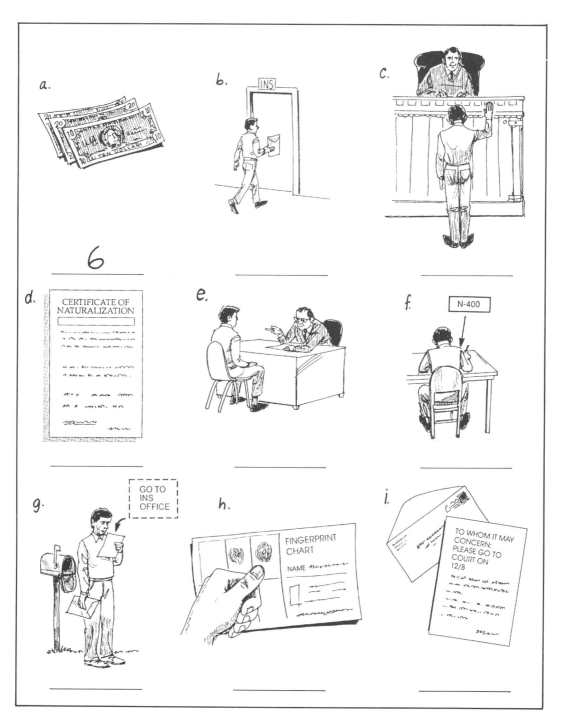

Write a short sentence about each picture.

1) _____

2) _____

3) _____

4) _____

5) _____

6) _____

7) _____

8) _____

9) _____

E. National Symbols. Write the names of the symbols under the pictures.

_____   _____   _____

_____   _____   _____

_____   _____   _____

Now circle the names of the symbols in the puzzle below. The first one is done for you.

```
W  A  S  H  I  N  G  T  O  N  M  O  N  U  M  E  N  T
H  I  T  O  M  P  U  K  L  E  J  F  W  A  Y  D  T  I
I  N  A  T  I  O  N  A  L  A  R  C  H  I  V  E  S  L
T  O  T  D  S  C  E  R  D  E  F  Z  O  L  A  B  I  U
E  F  U  S  C  A  P  I  T  O  L  A  L  D  O  I  P  A
H  A  E  K  I  N  U  R  E  R  A  P  S  R  A  M  U  R
O  Z  O  R  T  Y  D  I  N  O  G  J  F  M  E  M  T  O
U  R  F  W  A  H  I  N  T  E  R  N  M  C  L  I  N  B
S  E  L  I  N  C  O  L  N  M  E  M  O  R  I  A  L  S
E  H  I  N  D  E  P  E  N  D  E  N  C  E  H  A  L  L
L  I  B  E  R  T  Y  B  E  L  L  D  A  N  I  B  O  S
A  P  E  G  G  Y  M  A  L  L  I  E  M  K  O  L  V  I
R  E  R  S  T  R  A  M  E  M  O  N  P  A  R  D  N  G
B  U  T  S  A  L  L  E  N  E  M  O  H  A  T  R  Y  E
U  O  Y  N  I  K  K  I  A  N  N  L  B  E  D  S  O  C
```

Study Questions

After you finish this book, you should try to answer these questions. Be prepared to answer these questions when you go to INS for an examination.

BEING A U.S. CITIZEN

1. What kind of government does the U.S. have?
2. What official document tells the rules for the U.S. government?
3. Name one way citizens can help govern their community.
4. Name one advantage of being a U.S. citizen.
5. What is the most important right given to U.S. citizens?
6. How can a citizen become an informed voter?
7. Voting is one responsibility of a U.S. citizen. Name another responsibility.
8. Who makes the decision, guilty or not guilty, at most trials?
9. What do the stars represent on the U.S. flag?
10. What do the stripes represent on the U.S. flag?
11. What is the name of the U.S. President's official home?

THE NATURALIZATION PROCESS

1. Name two requirements for becoming a U.S. citizen.
2. What is the oath of citizenship?
3. Where do you go for a citizenship examination?
4. Tell one thing that happens at the final court hearing.

Vocabulary Index

Photo Credits

page 1—Architect of the Capitol

page 36—George Washington: Library of Congress
　　　　Abraham Lincoln: Library of Congress

page 125—UPI/Bettmann Newsphotos

page 157—Liberty Bell: Philadelphia Convention and Tourist Bureau
　　　　White House: Washington Convention and Visitors Bureau

page 158—Lincoln Memorial: Washington Convention and Visitors Bureau
　　　　U.S. Capitol: Washington Convention and Visitors Bureau

page 159—American Flag: Courtesy Michigan Travel Commission
　　　　Statue of Liberty: New York State Department of Commerce

page 160—Independence Hall: Standard Oil Company
　　　　Liberty Bell: Philadelphia Convention and Tourist Bureau

page 162—U.S. Capitol: Washington Convention and Visitors Bureau
　　　　White House: Washington Convention and Visitors Bureau
　　　　Washington Monument: Marc Anderson
　　　　Lincoln Memorial: Washington Convention and Visitors Bureau

page 163—Jefferson Memorial: Marc Anderson
　　　　National Archives: Washington Convention and Visitors Bureau

page 169—Independence Hall: Standard Oil Company
　　　　Statue of Liberty: New York State Department of Commerce
　　　　White House: Washington Convention and Visitors Bureau
　　　　Washington Monument: Marc Anderson
　　　　Liberty Bell: Philadelphia Convention and Tourist Bureau
　　　　National Archives: Washington Convention and Visitors Bureau

page 170—Lincoln Memorial: Washington Convention and Visitors Bureau
　　　　U.S. Capitol: Washington Convention and Visitors Bureau
　　　　American Flag: Courtesy Michigan Travel Commission